HOW
WINNERS
DO IT

HIGH IMPACT SKILLS FOR *YOUR* CAREER SUCCESS

MICHAEL W. MERCER, Ph.D.

PRENTICE HALL
Englewood Cliffs, New Jersey 07632

Prentice Hall International (UK) Limited, *London*
Prentice Hall of Australia Pty. Limited, *Sydney*
Prentice Hall Canada, Inc., *Toronto*
Prentice Hall Hispanoamericana, *S.A., Mexico*
Prentice Hall of India Private Limited, *New Dehli*
Prentice Hall of Japan, Inc., *Tokyo*
Simon & Schuster Asia Pte. Ltd., *Singapore*
Editora Prentice Hall do Brasil, Ltda., *Rio de Janeiro*

© 1994 *by*
Michael W. Mercer

10 9 8 7 6 5 4 3 2 1

Library of Congress Cataloging-in-Publication Data

Mercer, Michael W.
    How winners do it : high-impact skills for your career success /
Michael W. Mercer
        p. cm.
    Includes bibliographical references and index.
    ISBN 0-13-335704-X. -- ISBN 0-13-335696-5 (pbk.)
    1. Business communication.   2. Interpersonal communication.
3. Success in business. I. Title.
HF5718.M47   1994
650.14--dc20   93-46384
                                                              CIP

ISBN 0-13-335704-X
ISBN 0-13-335696-5 (pbk.)

Prentice Hall
Career & Personal Development
Englewood Cliffs, NJ 07632

Simon & Schuster, A Paramount Communications Company

Printed in the United States of America

To My Family,

My mother and father, Rhea and Philip
My sister and brother, Meridith and Jeffrey
My aunt, Idelle

ACKNOWLEDGMENTS

A number of people have helped make the conception, development, and writing of this book an exhilarating experience. I am tremendously grateful to them.

To begin, I greatly thank the many individuals who participated in my research on factors separating high-achievers from underachievers.

Also, I thank the many companies and business associations that invited me to deliver my keynote speeches and workshops to their members. These presentations allowed me to share the high-impact people skills with thousands of people who can benefit from them.

My dear friends the late Vincent J. McNamara, Joseph E. Troiani, and Maryann V. Troiani turned out to be the most magnificent cheerleaders any author could hope for. Their nonstop encouragement helped buoy me up throughout this writing project, as well as the growth of my training and consulting firm.

In addition, without Ellen Coleman and Jeffrey Herman, this book would not have been possible. I truly appreciate the roles they played.

Also, I feel grateful for the friendship of two other people: Robert W. Cormack not only continually helps me expand my preemployment testing business, he also is a constant source of joy with his delightful positive mental attitude. Plus, Bruno Cortis, a fantastic person to have as a friend.

TABLE OF CONTENTS

Acknowledgments iv

Introduction 1

    Research Reveals How Winners Do It 2

    Top 6 High-Impact Skills 5

    What This Book Will Help You Accomplish 8

High-Impact Skill 1
How to Make a Great Impression 11

    How to Make People Comfortable With You 11

        Look for the Similarities 14

        Heave the "Golden Rule" Out the Window 14

        Reap Tremendous Benefits When You Use the "Platinum Rule" 15

    6 Ways to Hit It Off with Practically Everyone 15

        Technique 1: Recognize and Reflect the 4 Interpersonal Styles 16

        Technique 2: Mirror, Mirror—Reflect What You See and Hear... 24

        Technique 3: Listen Attentively—It Makes a Powerful Impression 38

    What About the "Real" You? 41

        Technique 4: Engage in Artful Vagueness—The Winner's Way Out of a Sticky Situation 43

        Technique 5: Use Everyone's Favorite Word— Their Name 48

        Technique 6: Pay Three Compliments a Day 49

    Checklist—How to Make a Great Impression 51

High-Impact Skill 2
How to Negotiate, Influence, and Persuade
Like a Winner 53

Win-Win: The Best Possible Result 53

Two-Step Negotiating Method 54

3 Winning Persuasion Skills 56

Persuasion Skill 1: Ask for What You Want 56

Persuasion Skill 2: Adopt the Pace-and-Then-Lead Technique 57

Persuasion Skill 3: Ask the "Right" Questions 58

How to Get People into the Habit of Agreeing with You 63

How to Use the "Or" Technique to Get Action 65

2-Step Method to Overcome Resistance 66

One Word Winners Should Never Use 69

More Surefire Negotiating Techniques 71

Robin Hood 71

Time Is on Your Side 74

Brainstorming 76

Tom Sawyer 76

Fait Accompli *Approach 77*

The "Higher Authority" 78

The Back Burner 79

The FBI Technique 80

The Ultimatum 80

Vanish: An Ideal Technique When Only You *Can Make the Deal 81*

Backscratching—The Oldest Technique in the Book 83

The Dangers of Verbal Agreements 83

How to Conclude Every Negotiation 85

Checklist—How to Negotiate, Influence,
and Persuade 86

High-Impact Skill 3
Showmanship—How to Use Action and Interpersonal
"Theater" to Forge Ahead 89

Attitudes Are Contagious—Accentuate
the Positive 89

Exude Confidence 93

Delete This Word from Your Vocabulary 95
Join the Team 96

Assume Ultra-Responsibility 97

Publicize Your Successes 98

Touchy Topics—Career-Limiting Moves 100

Never Relieve Your Own Stress by Stressing Others 104

Pay 3 Sincere Compliments Each Day 106

Checklist—Showmanship—How to Use Action and
Interpersonal "Theater" to Forge Ahead 107

High-Impact Skill 4
How to Deliver Presentations That Impress 109

How Dynamic Presentations Can Open Doors
for You 110

3 Guaranteed Ways to Feel Calm and Confident 112

"Heavy Breathing" to Relieve Pressure 113
"Proud Hands" Technique to Create Buoyant
Confidence 113

One Simple, Yet Profound, Truth That Will Eliminate Nervousness 115

3 Quick Ways to Prepare Great Presentations 116

"Read" Your Audience's Needs and Desires 116

Organize Your Presentation in 30 Minutes or Less—Guaranteed 119

Create Visual Aids That Stand Out 120

The 3 DOs of First-Rate Presentations 124

DO—Move Your Body 124

DO—Use Your Voice for Maximum Impact 125

DO—Copy Professional Speakers 125

How to Tackle Difficult Questions, Comments, and Hard-to-Please Audience Members 126

How to Adeptly Handle Difficult Questions 127

How to Smoothly Handle Negative Comments 127

Secrets of Diplomatically Handling Hard-to-Please Audience Members 129

How to Encourage and Control Audience Participation 131

What *Not* to Say 132

How to Succeed at Giving the 2 Main Types of Presentations 134

Informative Presentations 134

Persuasive Presentations 135

Checklist—How to Deliver Presentations That Impress 137

High-Impact Skill 5
How to Conduct Highly Productive Meetings 139

What Is a Meeting? 140

Improving Your Organization's Bottom Line—
The Main Reason for Most Meetings 141

Characteristics of a Highly Productive Meeting 144

5 Steps to a Successful Meeting 145

Step 1: Plan the Meeting 145

Step 2: Organize the Agenda 147

Step 3: Conduct the Meeting 148

Step 4: Conclude the Meeting 160

Step 5: Postmeeting Follow-up 161

Checklist—How to Conduct Highly Productive
Meetings 162

High-Impact Skill 6
How to Develop Business Writing Skills 163

How to Write Crisp, Clear Memos, Letters, and
Reports Quickly 163

Do You Realize How Very Expensive Business
Writing Really Is? 164

Why Do So Many People Hate to Write? 166

How to Make Your Business Writing *Look* Like a
Winner 167

The First Step Toward Good Writing: "Read"
Your Reader's Needs and Desires 167

How to Write Faster and Better
(Plus Enjoy It More) 171

Everything You Always Wanted to Know About How to Write Like a Winner 172

Technique 1: Speeded Up Outlining 173

Technique 2: K.I.S.S. Your Reader 175

Technique 3: Vibrate with Vibrant Words 176

Technique 4: Add Color with Choice Words and Phrases 181

Technique 5: Plug in Words That Focus on Your Reader's Needs 182

Technique 6: P.S.: A Great Attention-Getter 184

Technique 7: Underline—It Eases Your Reader's Job...and Yours 184

Technique 8: Add Clarity with Subtitles 185

Technique 9: Benefit from Bullets—As Easy as 1-2-3 186

Technique 10: Create Visual Impact 187

How to Excel at the 2 Types of Business Writing 188

Informative Writing Techniques 188

Persuasive Writing Techniques 189

Checklist—Good Business Writing Made Easy 193

Conclusion
Tactics to Push Your Success to New Heights 195

It's Now Up to You 196

How to Improve Your High-Impact People Skills 197

Checklist—Plan and Improve Your High-Impact Skills 198

Now You Can Do It How Winners Do It 200

Appendix
How Companies Can Help Their Employees Excel 201

How to Pinpoint Exactly Which Skills Are Needed 201

Profiting from Psychological Assessments of Career Potential 202

Sample Psychological Assessment of Career Potential 204

Benefiting from Management Development Planning Meetings 212

What Are MDP Meetings 212

What Goes on in MDP Meetings? 213

Sample Management Development Planning Meeting Evaluation and Follow-up 213

How to *Really* Help Employees Through Performance Appraisals 216

Sample Performance Appraisal 217

Index 221

INTRODUCTION

Before I began my professional and business career, I had so little money that I could barely afford to buy food. So, I used to go to markets and *look* at the food. But, I didn't just go to *any* food store. Instead, I would walk around the fanciest and most expensive supermarket in one of the most fashionable neighborhoods in Chicago. I hungrily examined all the luscious food, gloriously displayed on the store's shelves and refrigerators. I had so little money that the most I could afford were the dented cans in the "sale" bins.

At the same time, I looked admiringly at the highly successful, beautifully dressed men and women who shopped in this supermarket. And I kept saying to myself that someday I would be able to walk into this store and buy whatever I wanted. I vowed that I would find out how highly successful people achieved their success so I could live like they did: dress nicely, buy whatever I desired without budgeting, and live in a fine home in a good neighborhood.

As I began my professional and business career, I focused on uncovering what separated the high-achievers from the underachievers. Fortunately, I chose a career path that has allowed me to earn my living while continually learning more and more about how winners do it.

RESEARCH REVEALS HOW WINNERS DO IT

Now, I'd like to let you in on how the entire *How Winners Do It* approach evolved. A number of companies approached me and said they had many employees who were intelligent and well educated. Some of them moved ahead very quickly to high-level management positions—either officers in divisions or high-level department directors or even vice presidents or presidents of companies. You might call those people high-achievers.

However, other equally intelligent and equally well educated employees were just not moving ahead as quickly or as well as their high-achieving colleagues. These companies asked me to

1. find out what differences existed between the groups
2. develop workshops or seminars to help the under-achievers become more similar to the high-achievers

But, before I started developing the workshops, I decided I needed to uncover specifically how winners do it—to find out how the high-achievers outperform their under-achieving colleagues or peers.

I conducted the research using three main methods:

* Interviewing executives
* "Shadowing" and observing high-achievers and under-achievers
* Reviewing test results of high-achievers and under-achievers

First, I interviewed executives, namely, the executives responsible for promoting—or not promoting—these people. I posed one key question to them: "Please tell me why some of the people you have working for you are high-achievers— people soaring ahead quickly to high-level management or professional positions—and why other people who are equally intelligent and equally educated (you might say your underachievers) do not move ahead nearly as well?"

At first, the executives found it difficult to explain this phenomenon. But, after they started thinking about it, most of them spoke with me at length about what separated the high-achievers from the underachievers. As I took notes during these interviews, I realized that some of the same skills used to describe the high-achievers were being mentioned over and over again.

Next, I asked the executives to give me names of some high-achievers and underachievers who worked for them. I then proceeded to tag along with or "shadow" these individuals. With many, I spent an entire day with them. I followed them, and observed how they acted. I sat next to them in meetings. I sat next to them in their offices and watched how they worked, handled phone calls, wrote correspondence and reports. I walked down corridors with them and watched how they interacted with people. I ate lunch with them. I enjoyed coffee breaks and chatting with them. I did everything with them throughout the day. In doing this, I noticed distinct differences in the ways high-achievers and under-achievers acted.

Finally, I looked at test results that assessed a person's behavior on the job *plus* their mental abilities. As an industrial psychologist, I do a lot of preemployment testing. That's testing job candidates to help companies predict—or forecast—which candidate will perform best on the job.

I then reviewed the results of testing that I had done over a period of years. I had tested thousands of job candidates. I looked at the test results of people I knew had zoomed ahead and soared to high-level management and executive positions.

I also analyzed test results of people I knew did not do nearly as well. They may have been equally intelligent and equally educated, but they just failed to advance as well.

In other words, I studied the test results of many high-achievers, as well as those of numerous underachievers. I reviewed test results that assessed these people's behavior on the job, namely, their interpersonal skills, personality traits, and motivations. I also inspected test results on their mental abilities.

All in all, I have done a lot of research on what separates high-achievers from underachievers.

When I analyzed all this information from interviews of executives, "shadowing" high- and underachievers and studying test results, I discovered the high-achievers consistently excelled at using six key interpersonal skills. I call them "high-impact skills."

Then, I went back to the executives I interviewed and asked them to arrange these six skills according to their order of importance. Skill 1 was the one they considered most important or of the highest priority, skill 2 the second most crucial, all the way down to skill 6, the one the executives considered the least important of these top six skills. These skills are, briefly, the ability to

1. Quickly make a fantastic impression on practically anyone: Charm.

2. Smoothly negotiate, influence, and persuade: Salesmanship.

3. Use actions and interpersonal "theater" to forge ahead: Showmanship.

4. Deliver impressive presentations.

5. Conduct highly productive meetings: Ringmaster.
6. Write crisp, clear memos, letters, and reports.

TOP 6 HIGH-IMPACT SKILLS

Now, let me expand on these high-impact skills. The first skill, the one at which high-achievers excel, is the ability to very quickly make a great impression on practically anyone. I call that *charm*. High-achievers are literally charming.

They very quickly develop rapport and a sense of camaraderie. These high-achievers readily help people feel comfortable with them. More important, they create a very good impression on the people who can make or break their careers, as well as a wide array of other people with whom they interact throughout their workday.

The second top people skill of high-achievers is their ability to smoothly and diplomatically persuade, influence, and negotiate. I call that *salesmanship*. Even if the high-achievers are not in sales or marketing positions, it is always quite important for them to "sell."

Think about it: All of us, regardless of the work we do, essentially are "salespeople." This significant point is illustrated each year when *Success* magazine features an entire monthly issue devoted to selling. Gloriously, and so very aptly, *Success*'s theme for this issue has been "Everyone Sells!" That proves so true! *Every* successful person sells every single day.

I also know the importance of this from my experience developing my training and consulting business. When I first left a corporate management position, I felt I was a professional who just happened to need to sell my services. However, I did not start achieving success in my business until I shifted my thinking and realized that actually I am a salesperson who just happens to offer professional services and products. What a mind shift!! And what a huge difference in my level of success it helped me create.

All of us must sell our services, ideas, and abilities. And if we work in sales, we even market actual products or services. That's why our ability to persuade, influence, and negotiate—so people will want to promote us or give us career opportunities—proves incredibly important. And high-achievers use such persuasion skills amazingly well.

The third skill used by high-achievers is what I call *showmanship*. By accompanying, or "shadowing," these high-achievers and underachievers, I discovered that high-achievers tend to act differently than their underachieving colleagues. You might say the high-achievers exude a different sense of interpersonal drama or theater in the ways they interact with other people. In other words, "showmanship."

Fourth, high-achievers excel at conducting highly productive meetings. They act like top-notch *ringmasters* or emcees. When people leave their meetings, they know exactly what to do. They feel motivated. No one feels they wasted time attending the meeting.

The fifth skill high-achievers possess is the ability to deliver impressive presentations to pretty much any size audience. Interestingly, skills 4 and 5—conducting highly productive meetings and delivering impressive presentations—actually go together. How? In entry-level jobs, or the early stages of our careers, we typically participate in other people's meetings and also attend presentations given by other people. As we move up the career ladder, we increasingly are the person conducting the meetings and delivering the presentations. Other people attend our meetings and sit in on our presentations. Clearly, the two key skills are mighty necessary to career growth.

In addition, the two skills always lead people to evaluate you, either positively or negatively, simply because they are high visibility skills. For instance, when you conduct a meeting, a number of people participate, all of whom develop an impression of you and your talents—or lack, thereof. The same holds true for audiences who attend your presentations.

Finally, the sixth skill I found that separates high-achievers from the underachievers is high-achievers' ability to write in a crisper, clearer, and more interesting manner. Their memos, letters, and reports—typical business writing—are livelier and more interesting. In fact, I observed something intriguing when I timed high-achievers and underachievers as they wrote: In general, I found high-achievers not only wrote more crisply and clearly, they also wrote more quickly.

What does all this boil down to? Well, it boils down to this very simple principle behind how winners do it:

Being competent in your work
plus 75 cents
will get you a cup of coffee.

Being competent in your work
plus making a fantastic impression on the people who count
will get you at least $100,000 per year.

Obviously, $100,000 per year is a metaphor. Some people who do exceedingly well in their careers make less, and some people earn vastly greater sums of money. But the principle behind it is quite clear: To get ahead, you must make a fantastic impression on the people who can make or break your career. These key people are the executives or managers who can offer you career opportunities or promotions. They also include the customers, clients, or patients who can give you business. When—and only when—you make a good impression on them, can you forge ahead in your career.

Another way to look at it is to realize that in lower-level or entry-level jobs, technical skills usually matter most. These are the skills needed to carry out the technical aspects of your job. Of less importance at this early stage are your people skills. After all, most people are initially hired for their technical knowledge, skills, or abilities.

For example, a company hires an entry-level accountant mainly to do technical accounting work. An engineer gets hired to do technical engineering work. But, as you move up in your career, your people skills count more and more.

After all, making a great impression on people very quickly, or being able to smoothly and diplomatically persuade, influence, and negotiate, are people skills—not technical skills. Showmanship most definitely is a people skill—a type of interpersonal drama or theater—in the way high-achievers tend to act. Conducting highly productive meetings, plus delivering impressive presentations also are people or communication skills. Writing in a crisp, clear interesting manner when you compose memos, letters, and reports illustrates yet another type of communication skill. All in all, *making a fantastic impression on the people who can make or break your career counts a great deal.*

WHAT THIS BOOK WILL HELP YOU ACCOMPLISH

It all boils down to this: *style* and *impact*. Specifically, what counts most is the *style* with which you do things and the *impact* you have on the people who can make or break your career.

In *How Winners Do It*, I explain and illustrate specific techniques used by high-achievers. I will let you in on the crucial interpersonal and communication skills that you need to surge ahead in your career. You will discover

* Powerful methods for persuading and influencing
* Surefire negotiating tactics
* The key to making a great impression on just about everyone you meet
* How to use "showmanship" to your advantage
* What to do to deliver dynamic presentations and conduct highly productive meetings
* Ready-to-use techniques that make good business writing incredibly easy and fast

You will learn the secrets of how winners do it so you, too, can become a high-achiever. In fact, by using these methods, you can *exceed* the expectations of many people who can make—or break—your career. You too can be a winner.

High-
Impact **1**
Skill

HOW TO MAKE
A GREAT IMPRESSION

In this chapter, we delve into high-impact skill 1, that is, quickly making a great impression on practically anyone.

At the same time, we will look at the first step of how to excel in using the high-impact skill 2, namely, how to negotiate, influence, and persuade smoothly and diplomatically.

HOW TO MAKE PEOPLE COMFORTABLE WITH YOU

The first step in persuading, influencing, and negotiating requires that you get people to feel comfortable with you. To accomplish this first step in negotiating, you must first make a good impression.

To illustrate, try this: *Imagine* somebody with whom you feel extremely *un*comfortable. This person really does not seem to understand you or be on your wavelength. You definitely feel out of sync with this person.

Next, imagine that this person tries to persuade you to do something. On a scale of 1 through 10—where 1 is very

11

low and 10 is very high—how likely is it that you *might* be persuaded by this person with whom you feel mighty uncomfortable?

I asked this question of hundreds of people. Ninety-nine times out of a 100, they estimated the likelihood that they would be persuaded to be only 1, 2, or 3, occasionally 4, obviously, quite low. This demonstrates that it would be very difficult for most people to succeed in persuading someone who felt uncomfortable with them to do or agree to anything.

Think of someone with whom you typically do not get along. Isn't it true that as soon as this person even tries to persuade you to do something, a spark ignites in your brain and you begin to conjure up reasons why you do not agree or "cannot" do what that person wants. In fact, you probably start ticking off reasons in your mind to squirm out of getting persuaded—even before the person finishes making his or her pitch to you.

Now, let's switch our focus and do this: Picture another person with whom you feel very comfortable. You feel this person certainly is in sync with you. You sense this person definitely is on your wavelength. In addition you feel confident that this person completely understands your thoughts, needs, feelings, and opinions.

With this delightful person in your mind, please answer this question: On the same scale of 1 through 10—where 1 is very low and 10 is very high—how likely are you to maybe be persuaded by this person with whom you feel so incredibly comfortable?

I asked this question of hundreds of people. Their responses invariably were 7, 8, 9, and sometimes even 10. This points out a basic fact of human nature:

People are much more likely to be persuaded
by someone with whom they feel comfortable than
by someone with whom they feel uncomfortable.

It is pretty hard to influence anybody who feels *un*comfortable with you. After all, most people resist being persuaded by someone they are not comfortable with. They conjure up abundant excuses to escape being convinced or swayed by somebody they feel uncomfortable with.

How do we describe someone we feel comfortable with? We might say to ourselves,

> "I feel really comfortable with you. I feel we're in sync."
>
> "It's wonderful how comfortable I feel with you. I feel like we're both on the same wavelength."
>
> "I feel so comfortable with you. You really understand my thoughts, needs, feelings, and opinions."

That's what comfort with another human being boils down to—feeling like you're (1) in sync, (2) on the same wavelength or, at the very least, (3) the person understands your thoughts, needs, feelings, and opinions.

Comfort Indicators

Feeling comfortable with another human being boils down to a

* Feeling you are *in sync*
* Sensing you are *on the same wavelength*
* Noticing the other person *understands you*, especially your

 Thoughts
 Needs
 Feelings
 Opinions

Look for the Similarities

Given these totally natural, deeply human reactions, the basic principle behind making people feel comfortable with you also offers you the basic principle behind making a great impression on practically anyone:

Human beings want to be around people
who seem similar to themselves.

What is the key word in this key principle? The key word is *seem*.

In all truthfulness, everyone is different from everyone else in at least a thousand different ways. In fact, if you think of all the people you know, you most likely have hundreds of thousands—maybe even millions—of differences with your friends, colleagues, and acquaintances.

However, you get along with them to some degree, because you determine how you *seem* similar with each of those many people. For instance, you may have some similar

* Interests
* Thoughts
* Needs
* Feelings
* Experiences
* Goals

So, you search for some ways in which you *seem* similar to other people so you can get along with them.

Heave the "Golden Rule" Out the Window

Very important, given the fact that human beings do crave to be around people who *seem* similar to themselves, avoid wasting your time on the widespread fantasy that you could make people feel extremely comfortable with you by using the "Golden Rule." The Golden Rule states, "Treat other people as *you* want to be treated." Reason: Because, in their innermost yearnings, most people really do not want to be treated the way *you* want to be treated.

Instead, almost everyone craves to be treated the way *they* like being treated—*not* the way *you* want to be treated.

Reap Tremendous Benefits When You Use the "Platinum Rule"

Instead of using the "Golden Rule," help people feel vastly more comfortable with you—and quickly make a good impression—by using the "Platinum Rule." The Platinum Rule asserts,

Treat other people the way they like being treated.

By doing that, most people will like you and feel comfortable with you. Or, at the very least, you will make a much better impression than when you focus chiefly on *your* likes and dislikes by treating them the way *you* want to be treated.

Just as platinum is more valuable than gold, the "Platinum Rule" helps you hurry along your road to success much more easily and quickly than the "Golden Rule." That explains why platinum proves much more valuable than gold in human affairs, as well as in financial affairs.

6 WAYS TO HIT IT OFF
WITH PRACTICALLY EVERYONE

Now, let's look at how winners quickly make great impressions on practically everyone they meet.

***Technique 1: Recognize and Reflect
the 4 Interpersonal Styles***

The first rapport-generating technique is what I call the "4 Interpersonal Styles." Basically, there are only four main ways in which people interact or deal with one another. As I describe each style, just imagine people you know who— more or less—fit into each of the four styles.

Four Interpersonal Styles

TASK- MORE THAN PEOPLE-ORIENTED

	RESULTS-FOCUSED "*Quickly* tell me what time it is, *not* how to build a clock!!!!"	DETAIL-FOCUSED "*Slowly* tell me how to build a clock, *slowly* leading up to what time it is."
PUSHY	PARTYING-FOCUSED "Sorry my backslapping was so hard, but you look so funny when you fall down. Wanna hear another joke? Let's PARTY!!!!"	FRIENDLY-FOCUSED "First, I'll tell you about my family [weekend, personal experiences]. Then let's talk about yours. Then, let's chat about the work we need to do."

PUSHY   **NOT PUSHY**

PEOPLE- MORE THAN TASK-ORIENTED

First is the *Results-Focused* person. People of this sort absolutely love you when you *very quickly*

* Walk into their office
* Say what you did
* Depart

To put it in a nutshell, the Results-Focused person delights in finding out "what time it is" *and* usually could not care less about how you build a clock.

The second type is the *Detail-Focused* person. In sharp contrast to the Results-Focused person, a Detail-Focused person wants to know all the little itsy-bitsy, teeny-weeny details of how you build a clock. *And*, in fact, the Detail-Focused person may not give a hoot about what time it is.

Detail-Focused people relish your visit when you

* Carefully walk into their office with a pile of papers or data to discuss
* Sit down like you plan to remain quite awhile
* Slowly and carefully plod through all the little details of what you did
* Slowly and carefully go through all the small details of what you plan to do.

Throughout your conversation, you need to help reassure the Detail-Focused person, make her feel comfortable that every single little deed you did and will do definitely will work absolutely perfectly. Why? Because Detail-Focused people are perfectionists.

I call the third type of person a *Friendly-Focused* person. When you go to see him—before he can get down to the work at hand—he first needs to talk about *his* weekend, family, and friends. And then, before he gets down to the work that must be done, he desires to talk about *your* weekend, family, and friends. And then he feels a craving to gossip about *someone else's* weekend, family, and friends.

After he gets all that friendly chit-chat out of his system, the Friendly-Focused person is willing to get down to brass tacks and discuss the work needing attention. At that point the Friendly-Focused person typically transforms into either a Results-Focused or Detail-Focused individual.

Finally, the fourth type of interpersonal style is somebody who uses a *Partying-Focused* approach. Partying-Focused people show up at work long enough to rest up and get another paycheck so they can go out and party some more. Partying-Focused people savor having a good time. They utterly cherish your presence when you laugh at their jokes and humor—even if you are the brunt of some of their jokes. They enjoy your existence on this planet even more if you tell them jokes, too.

In fact, you can detect a Partying-Focused person from about 50 feet down the corridor by all the laughter and raucousness and noise coming out of his office—even if he is there all by himself.

Not surprisingly, Partying-Focused people may do incredibly well when their family owns the business where they work.

Now the question arises: How do you greatly increase your odds of making a fantastic impression and comfortably getting along with each type of person?

To answer this question, we simply need to return to the basic principle behind (1) helping people feel comfortable with you and (2) making a great impression:

Human beings want to be around people
who seem similar to themselves.

Quick Quiz: 4 Interpersonal Styles

Question: What is the best way to impress a Results-Focused person? (Listen to the drum rolls as you come up with your answer.)

Answer: Act Results-Focused. Wow! Isn't that incredible? You simply need to act in such a way that you *seem* similar to the Results-Focused person. Just tell her what time it is, *not* how you built the clock.

Question: What happens if you want to help a Detail-Focused person feel at ease with the essence of your being?

Answer: Dive head first into all the little itsy-bitsy, teeny-weeny details of how to build the clock (you may never even get around to saying what time it actually is).

I bet you are catching on ultra-fast and earning an abundance of points in this tournament.

Question: How do you make a great impression on a Friendly-Focused person?

Answer: First, ask him about his weekend, family, and friends. Next, you tell him a bit about your weekend, family, and friends. And, if he has still not gotten the friendly chit-chat out of his system, indulge his longing to chatter by talking about someone else's life. After that, watch the Friendly-Focused person transform into either a Results-Focused or Detail-Focused person, and follow his lead.

And the final, last and deciding question to see if you really know the *4 Interpersonal Styles*:

Question: What do you do to make a fantastic impression on a Partying-Focused person?

Answer: You know the answer: First, always laugh at her jokes. Second, bring in some jokes of your own, because she loves to laugh, and if you make her laugh, she'll really prize your presence. If you do not know any jokes, or you have not yet mastered the art of witty conversation, use this surefire technique: Clip some cartoons out of a magazine or newspaper. A Partying-Focused person will love you for showing her anything that triggers a laugh or, at the very least, a smile.

How to Use the Interpersonal Styles Technique

Imagine that you are a Results-Focused person (even if you are not). Your main concern centers on "what time it is." You don't care how anyone "builds the clock."

Now, imagine that an extremely Detail-Focused person comes to see you. This person sits down as if he plans to spend a lot of time with you. He slowly tells you how he "built the clock," carefully telling you all the little details.

As a Results-Focused person, would you feel this Detail-Focused person

* seems in sync with you?
* acts as if he is on the same wavelength as you?
* really understands your thoughts, needs, feelings and opinions?

Of course not. In fact, you'd probably yearn to toss him out of your office. You may even suspect something is *wrong* with him. After all, he talks and does things so slowly! And it seems *so* incredibly hard to make the Detail-Focused person just get to the point he wants to make!!

Now, let's change the scenario. Imagine you are a very Detail-Focused person. An extremely Results-Focused person dashes into your office. She strides so quickly that you wonder if she even touches the ground as she walks. She *very quickly*

* Says what she did

* Tells you what she will do next

* Walks out before you can even say more than a few words

Would you feel like you're in sync with that Results-Focused person? As a very Detail-Focused person, would you feel like she is on the same wavelength as you? Would you even suspect this person fully understands your thoughts, needs, feelings, and opinions?

Probably not. In fact, you may even think something seems peculiar about that person. She does everything *so* rapidly. You might even speculate that she is trying to hide things from you. Or, as a "fast-talker," maybe she is even attempting to con you (after all, cons often are fast-talkers!).

The central idea boils down to this: The Results-Focused person is not great or lousy, and the Detail-Focused person is not great or lousy. What matters most is

Human beings want to be around people
who seem similar to themselves.

That is, people prefer to deal with someone who employs the Platinum Rule:

Treat others as they like being treated.

TIP: HOW TO IMPRESS A VERY NERVOUS PERSON. Keep in mind that when someone feels nervous or tense, he or she almost invariably acts Detail-Focused. That occurs just as naturally as spring follows winter. That is because a wound-up person frets that something may go haywire. Think about this: How do you make sure nothing goes wrong? Most people do it by becoming Detail-Focused, so they can make sure every *i* is dotted and every *t* is perfectly crossed. After all, if everything is perfect nothing can go wrong.

Given this situation, when you find yourself with an anxious soul, make sure each and every little itsy-bitsy, teeny-weeny detail is totally flawless. Check (and double check and triple check) that everything appears correct. By cautiously acting perfectionistic, nothing can go wrong, and therefore, the nervous, Detail-Focused person has nothing left to worry about. That helps a highly nervous spirit feel somewhat more serene.

Fast Rehearsals That Will Help You Hit It Off with Anyone

What should you do? Just follow these four guidelines:

* When you see a Results-Focused person, act results-focused.

* When you see a Detail-Focused person, act detail-focused.

* When you see a Friendly-Focused person, act friendly-focused.

* When you see a Partying-Focused person, act partying-focused.

Now, let's do a little mental calisthenics to help you practice using these four interpersonal styles. Please picture somebody you know who is *results-focused*, somebody you know who mainly wants to know what time it is. This person does not care about all the good work you did building the clock that will tell him what time it is.

What could you do to seem a little bit more like that Results-Focused person? How could you appear to be

* a bit speedier?
* more results-focused?
* a little more like a "bottom-line" sort of person?

Let's switch gears: Think of somebody who is *detail-focused*. This is a person who wants you to

* Spend a lot of time with him
* Tell (in extremely excruciating detail) her how you built the clock *and* how you plan to build the next clock *and* assure her that each clock will work perfectly

Even if you do not typically act detail-focused, what specific actions could you take to make that person feel like you *seem* on the same wavelength or in sync? That is, how could you *act* more detail-focused with that person?

Next, imagine someone you know who is *friendly-focused*. This is one human animal who loves to chit-chat. Before he get down to discussing work, he wants to talk about personal things. Even if you tend not to be friendly-focused, what specific behaviors could you use to make that Friendly-Focused person feel "at home" with you?

Finally, picture somebody you know who oozes a *partying-focused* style. She loves to laugh and have a good time. What can you do to make that Partying-Focused person feel like you are at least somewhat like her?

By answering these questions about *specific actions* you could take to make each type of person feel more comfortable, more in sync and more on the same wavelength with you—you will discover how you can make a great impression on a wide variety of people

* very quickly
* very subtly

Technique 2: Mirror, Mirror— Reflect What You See and Hear . . .

The second technique that helps make a great impression on people is mirroring. This is an incredibly subtle yet powerful way to use certain key habits of the person you want to impress in order to help that person subconsciously feel comfortable with you.

By recognizing specific habits a person uses, and then using some of those same habits when interacting with the person, you automatically put the Platinum Rule into action: You are *subtly* treating the person as he or she likes being treated.

Specifically, you can mirror—or make yourself seem similar to—someone in terms of their

* Body language
* Vocal style
* Formality of attire

By mirroring these behaviors, you leave the person with an implicit sense that you are like him or her; that is, you *seem* in sync or on the same wavelength.

How to Mirror Body Language

The most basic mirroring technique you can use is to mirror a person's body language. When done well, you can very quickly induce someone to feel comfortable with you.

Consider this example. Imagine you are sitting down and somebody comes up to you and hovers over you—actually peers down at you. He then tries to hold a conversation with you.

How would you feel at that moment? Would you feel you were on the same wavelength, in sync, or comfortable with that person? Undoubtedly, your answer is a resounding, "No! Of course not!" Very few people find that situation comfortable. Instead, you may feel that person is trying to one-up you or take a "power" position over you.

Next, imagine that same person sitting down in a chair just a few feet from yours, faced toward you. You instantly would start feeling a little bit more comfortable with that person, because his body language—sitting—is similar to your body language, which is sitting, too.

How would you feel if you leaned back in your chair and the other person leaned forward, almost into your face? Would you feel comfortable with that person then? Probably not. By jutting forward, this person encroaches on your space and is not physically on the same wavelength as you.[1] The important fact here is that this person is not mirroring you.

Now, imagine that you lean back, while the other person also leans back. You probably would feel somewhat more comfortable almost immediately because this person's body language is mirroring yours.

Think of a time you leaned forward very excitedly telling someone about something, but that person leaned back, perhaps as though she wanted no part of it. Her body language left you with the impression she was not very inter-

---

[1]I act out body language scenarios in my *How Winners Do It* and *Negotiating* workshops. Once, when I purposely stood very close to a seated workshop participant, she colorfully exclaimed, "You're intruding on my aura!"

ested in what you were saying. At the very least, she appeared less involved and enthusiastic than you felt.

Now, imagine you feel very enthusiastic and you lean forward at a 45-degree angle eagerly telling somebody about this thing that excites you. The person you are talking to also leans toward you at a *similar* 45-degree angle. She *seems* involved in what you are saying. Since both of you are leaning forward, you would feel fairly comfortable with that person. Why? Because your body language *seems* to indicate you are in sync with one another.

These commonplace examples of you and another person standing or sitting, or leaning forward or back, show you how powerful yet subtle mirroring can be. If you want to make a good impression on someone, it works wonders to mirror his or her movements.

Here's how you can do it:

First, you can mirror the person's *standing posture*. If she stands, you stand, too. If she leans a bit or perhaps leans on a table, then you lean a bit, also. If she stands superstraight and stiff as a board, then you, too, can by standing straight and stiff as a board.

You can also mirror other people's *sitting posture*. If she sits leaning back, you also can lean back. If she sits leaning forward, you might lean forward a bit.

Caveat emptor: Be careful when you mirror someone's body language that you *avoid mimicking* the person. Think about when you were five years old, and you wanted to get on another child's nerves. The guaranteed fastest method—it took only 5 minutes or less—was for you to mimic the other child all the way down to the smallest detail. When you did this, you soon managed to get the other child very upset. At that point, the object of your mimicking might start screaming, yelling, complaining, or crying about the torture you were inflicting by mimicking his or her body language or speech.

As an adult, if your goal is to make someone comfortable with you, you do not want to get anywhere near that extreme. You just want to subtly mirror the person you want to impress; to appear *somewhat* like that person, not be a carbon copy of the person.

Another technique, in addition to mirroring posture, is to mirror *movements*. For example, think about people you know who talk with their hands. When they talk, their hands go all over the place. It is almost as if they are literally "talking" with their hands.

In such cases, discomfort can erupt when a person who talks with her hands converses with someone who keeps his hands almost glued to his sides. Think about it. Given their hand movements, do these two people seem to be on the same wavelength? Certainly not. One probably feels the other person is too reserved. Meanwhile, that supposedly reserved person feels sure the person who talks with her hands is overly dramatic or emotional.

A No-Holds-Barred Case of How Mirroring Works Wonders
I will tell you of the situation that startled me into realizing the subtle potency inherent in mirroring body language of someone I want to impress. At one company where I held a management position, I worked hard doing the best job I could. I soon discovered that one of the top-level executives served as what you might call the career "gate keeper." That executive—let's call him Bob—played a key role in deciding which managers got promoted into upper-level management or executive positions.

This executive and I did not get along too well. Do not get me wrong. We did not snap at each other—we simply did not feel a sense of rapport or comfort with each other.

Fortunately, at about that time, I went to a workshop on communications skills where I discovered the value of mirroring. I also realized why Bob and I did not feel the sense of camaraderie so necessary if I was to impress him so he would want to help my career. Before I tell you the solution I reached, you need to understand what happened every time I went to see Bob. I would walk into his office, and almost immediately Bob would stand up, walk to his office window, and look out the window while talking to me. Then, Bob would sit on a table located next to the window, and after that, would walk to his desk and sit on it. Then, he would move behind his desk where he would sit, feet up on his desk. Next, he would pick himself up, and again walk over to the window. Bob was in almost constant motion, never staying still for more than a minute. He moved around nonstop. In fact, it almost seemed as if he were doing aerobics during our meetings.

Throughout, I would sit in a chair with my back stiff as a board and one leg crossed over the other. I hoped my sitting posture would make me look very "professional." Unfortunately, Bob probably did not view it that way. After all, Bob was vigorously moving around his office as I sat looking stilted and restrained.

That explained our problem. Of course, we did not get along well. Our body language really was absurdly out of sync.

The day after the workshop where I learned about mirroring body language, I had a meeting scheduled with Bob. I walked into his office feeling confident that I had finally figured out how to get along with him.

As I strode into his office, Bob immediately did what he always did: He stood up, and walked over to his window. Without delay, I walked over to the window, too. The two of us gazed out the window for a few minutes while chatting.

Then, Bob went over to the table, and sat down on it. I sat down on the table, too.

After a while, Bob went and sat on his desk. I walked over, too, and sat on Bob's desk.

Then, Bob sat down in his big executive chair, and put his feet up onto his desk, almost right in front of my face. I sat down in a chair next to his desk and put my feet up on it too. Then, Bob leaned far back in his chair—sort of like an astronaut sitting in a spaceship at take-off. I, too, leaned way back in my chair, just like Bob. In fact, I almost tumbled over backwards.

All this bustle continued for most of our half-hour meeting. But, most important, something clicked. Bob and I actually got along, and felt comfortable with each other.

As I left Bob's office, he enthusiastically remarked, "Mike, I'm looking forward to seeing you next week at the management meeting. We're really going to get a lot accomplished."

After I left Bob's office, I walked to my boss's office. When I arrived, my boss was on the phone. He motioned with his hand for me to enter. After a minute or two, he hung up his phone, and announced to me, "Mike, that was Bob on the phone. I don't know what you did, but he sure likes you. He says there's something about you that he really likes."

Then, he asked, "What did you do? You and Bob weren't getting along that well before. What did you do differently?"

I replied, "You wouldn't believe it if I told you." And he probably would not have. When people correctly mirror each other's body language, it is incredibly subtle. People tend not to notice it on a conscious level, because they so *habitually* move the way they do. Fortunately, however, they do notice at a subconscious, innate, or emotional level that they feel very comfortable with the person who *seems* to use somewhat similar body language.

The Power of Mirroring Is All Around You

Try this suggestion: The next time you feel great comfort and rapport with somebody, notice how you and the

other person are sitting or standing. It is quite likely that
both of you are sitting or standing or moving in a fairly similar manner.

When two people feel comfortable with one another,
they often naturally mirror each other. Reason: When you
feel close to someone, you literally, figuratively, and emotionally, "*seem* similar to that person." That explains why
you experience those wonderful, warm feelings of rapport.

Interestingly, studies show that if the first person a
newborn sees is his or her mother smiling, then the newborn
smiles, too. And if the newborn sees the mother frowning,
the newborn also frowns. It seems that even at a very early
age people instinctively know that mirroring others leads to
a feeling of comfort.

As a professional speaker and management consultant,
I very often deal with people I have never met before. At
first, I was self-conscious about what to do with my body.
After all, I have no choice: I *must* bring my body with me!
But I would wonder how I should move, stand, and sit when
meeting new people.

Mirroring helped me solve this problem. Now, when I
meet someone for the first time, I immediately start mirroring his or her body language. For instance, if she

* is standing, then I stand
* is sitting, I sit
* talks with her hands, I do likewise
* keeps her hands glued down to her sides, then I keep
  my hands glued down to my sides

Such instant mirroring helps the person I just met
quickly feel at least somewhat comfortable with me. In addition, I feel more comfortable, because I do not worry about

* what to do with my hands
* whether I should sit or stand
* how I should move

All in all, mirroring accelerates developing comfort, rapport, and interpersonal trust. It also makes our interactions and collaborations smoother, less stressful, and more likely to succeed.

TIP: HOW TO BENEFIT FROM MIRRORING IN MEETINGS You even can use mirroring to help get on the good side of someone at a meeting. For instance, at a meeting you may want to garner the attention, approval, or help of a particular person in the meeting. You know if that person feels comfortable with you, then the person will probably like you. Anyone who likes you is fairly likely to agree with you or express support for ideas you propose in the meeting.

To achieve this goal in a meeting, mirror the body language of the person whose approval or support you wish to acquire. As an example, if the person leans forward in his chair, then you lean forward in your chair, also. If the person leans back, then you lean back.

Plus, be absolutely sure to take one more highly useful, yet subtle, action: As the person speaks, nod your head up and down to convey agreement. Or silently mouth the words

* "Yes"
* "Right"
* "Good point"
* "I agree"

What reaction does this get? From a body language point of view, this person feels

✳ comfortable with you

✳ both of you are on the same wavelength

✳ you are in sync

Think about it: How do you feel toward someone who acts like she agrees with you? You feel favorably disposed toward that obviously wise and wonderful human being.

Given this typical reaction, mirroring another person's body language and mouthing words of agreement helps that person feel favorably disposed toward you, too. This positive reaction would prompt her to agree or be supportive when you speak in the meeting. That is what you want from people whenever you participate in a meeting, isn't it?

How to Mirror Vocal Style

Mirroring *vocal style* is another excellent mirroring technique. For example, some people talk loudly. Others talk softly. When you talk with someone, match the *volume* of that person's voice with your own.

In addition to volume, you can also mirror a person's *rate* or *speed* of speaking. Many people speak quickly. In fact, some people talk so rapidly they convey the impression they would prefer to communicate via mental telepathy rather than speaking.

At the other extreme, you find people who speak slowly. Some slow-talkers speak *so* slowly that fast-talkers cannot resist completing their sentences for them.

Interestingly, slow-talkers sometimes think fast-talkers are trying to put something over on them. After all, they are "fast-talkers" which is an idiom implying a con artist. On the other hand, many fast-talkers think slow-talkers are a bit dumb or "slow." In fact, one definition of the word "slow" in the dictionary is "dull-witted."

However, the fact remains: No one is good or bad for speaking softly or loudly, nor is any person good or bad for speaking quickly or slowly, but mirroring a person's speech pattern helps create a sense that you *seem* similar to that person.

To subtly make a good impression on someone, simply match the person's volume and rate of speech. For example, if a person speaks softly and quickly, then speak somewhat softly and quickly, even if that is not your typical speech pattern. You have nothing to lose and a lot to gain by mirroring another person's vocal style.

Another way to mirror vocal style centers on the *emotion* a voice conveys. Recall a time you felt dejected, awfully serious, concerned, or downright nervous, and somebody in a cheerful mood gushed, "Oh, it's not so bad. The world's great, and you're just too down on yourself."

Did you feel that gleeful character really understood your feelings? Probably not. Keep in mind that if someone is incredibly serious, perhaps even nervous or depressed, you do not need to act suicidal to get along with that person. But, in a sensitive way, you can lower your voice and talk to that person using a more serious tone of voice. By doing this, you sound more attuned to that person.

Now, picture a time you felt exuberant, happy, and wonderfully enthusiastic, and you ran into someone whose voice conveyed a sense of impending doom. Did you and that person seem to be on the same wavelength or in sync? I bet not. In fact, you probably needed to change the inflections in your voice to get along a bit better with that person.

These examples lead to a vital pointer:

To get along with people, mirror their vocal style.

For example, if they talk loudly, then you ought to talk somewhat loudly. When they talk as softly as a mouse, you need to talk softer. If they talk quickly, then you need to quicken your pace. When their words come out slowly, then speak slowly. If they sound happy and upbeat, you need to make your voice sound happy and upbeat. When the reverse occurs, work on sounding a trifle more serious.

As always,

> *Human beings want to be around people*
> *who seem similar to themselves.*

Somewhat mirroring someone's vocal style makes you *seem* more like that person. And while it is amazingly subtle, it is very easy to do.

How to Mirror Attire

A third mirroring technique you can use is to *mirror attire*. The first thing you see when you look at someone is how he or she looks. This includes how a person dresses.

To investigate the importance of mirroring attire, I conducted a quasi-scientific research project at an indoor shopping mall. The mall contains a food court with booths where shoppers can buy an array of refreshments or meals. After buying food, patrons can sit at any one of the 100 or so tables in the food court.

This mall's clientele consists of middle-class to upper-class people who tend to dress in two main ways: (1) preppy and (2) in the latest high-priced fashions.

I used this mall for my "research" into mirroring attire. I brought two catalogs:

* ❋ L. L. Bean, which features preppy garb

* ❋ Neiman-Marcus, which highlights the latest, most up-to-date fashions trends

I put the two catalogs on a table in the food court, and sat back at a nearby table to watch how shoppers responded.

The first people walking to that table dressed ultra-preppy. Guess which catalog they focused on. They took one look at the two catalogs and *immediately* dove into the L. L. Bean catalog.

When they left, I took the catalogs and plopped them down on another empty table. A few minutes later, a couple dressed in the latest trendy fashions sat there. I bet you know which catalog they chose. They glanced at the two catalogs for precisely one millisecond, and picked up the Neiman-Marcus catalog.

This "research" was so amusing that I continued it for a few hours. During that time, I observed dozens of people deciding which catalog to look at. *Without exception*, the results always were the same:

* The preppy dressers picked up the L. L. Bean catalog.
* Those wearing the latest, most up-to-date fashions always selected the Neiman-Marcus catalog.

This remarkably consistent finding suggests a profound truth: "Human beings want to be around people who *seem* similar to themselves." When given a choice, people opt to *look* at people who dress as they do, rather than people who dress differently.

To get the most mileage out of mirroring attire, remember you must *mirror the level of formality* of the clothes worn by the person you want to feel comfortable with you. For example, if you dress in formal business attire at work—maybe a very fine dress or suit—how would it strike you if someone showed up in jeans or other sports clothes? Even if that person were brilliant and highly competent, your first impression probably would be, "There's something a little bit out of sync between us. We have a *dis*similarity." After all, a formally dressed person may feel a twinge of uneasiness with the more informally decked-out individual.

A friend of mine once accepted an invitation to a cocktail party. The hostess was a woman my friend knew always dressed casually at social events she held. So, my friend confidently strode into the cocktail party wearing a sports coat. The instant he appeared in the doorway, everyone stopped talking for a moment and looked at him. All the guests at the cocktail party were wearing formal apparel. The women appeared splendid in their glorious evening gowns and spectacular jewelry. All the men wore dinner jackets—*except* my friend, who was horribly embarrassed. It seemed like a bad dream. His mistake lay in not bothering to read the invitation. It clearly stated the cocktail party was a "black tie" affair. In this case, his negligence resulted in a social blunder: not mirroring the required *formality* of attire.

Such a social *faux pas* does not mean that my friend is not a wonderful person or flourishing in his career. It also does not imply that everyone dressed formally is fabulous. But it does demonstrate that

> *Human beings want to be around people who*
> *seem—and dress—similar to themselves.*

And mirroring the level of formality of dress helps create this feeling.

To illustrate the effect of mirroring levels of formality in business, here is a description of several typical situations that occur when I go to a company to consult, conduct a workshop, or deliver a speech. The first people I usually speak to are top-level managers in the executive suite. I typically enter with my suit jacket on, my tie pulled securely up to my throat, and a starched white dress shirt. The moment I walk into the office, I look at the people I am encountering. If the men have their suit jackets on—or if the men and women are dressed in formal business attire—then I keep my jacket on.

If the men are not wearing their jackets—which is very common—I take mine off within five seconds. Why? It instantly makes me *seem* visually more like them.

What would happen if, for example, the men in the meeting had their suit jackets off, but I kept mine on? I would seem much more formal—perhaps even stuffier—than they. So, I simply remove my suit coat and I instantly appear a bit more in sync.

I may walk from the executive suite to visit the company's factory. Factory workers typically wear work clothes that can get dirty. They may even have grease or oil on their clothing. I certainly would not smear grease or dirt on my dress shirts.

However, to blend in better, before I walk into the factory, I take off my suit coat. Sometimes I even loosen my tie and roll up my shirt sleeves. Then, when I talk to the production supervisors or other people in the factory, I *seem* a little bit more like them. That is because I am mirroring their clothing's *level of formality*. Obviously, I am still wearing basically formal business attire—dress pants, dress shirt, and maybe a tie. But, by loosening my tie and rolling up my sleeves, I *seem* less formal or stuffy.

Then, before I return to the executive suite, I button my shirt, tighten my tie, and roll down my sleeves. And, if needed, I put on my suit jacket. Again, this helps me mirror the level of formality of the people I am dealing with in the executive suite.

TIP: BLANDING IN—THE UNWRITTEN DRESS CODE When you mirror attire to help people feel comfortable with you and to impress people, keep in mind that every company

* has a dress code
* almost always this dress code is unwritten

✳ quite often the dress code is not even openly discussed

In effect, the "dress code" is a metarule. But there always is a dress code that people who make a great impression discern and follow.

Let me illustrate this. When you go into most organizations, employees in lower-level jobs tend to dress heterogeneously. That is, they wear a variety of clothing styles and types.

In contrast, the high-level executives tend to dress rather homogeneously or rather like one another. This does not make any of these people better, more intelligent, or more able. It just reflects the principle that

Human beings want to be around people
who seem similar to themselves.

Often, employees who are very skilled in their jobs *and* move ahead in their careers also *look* capable to the executives who can give them career opportunities. One simple reason for that is these high-achievers dress somewhat like the executives they need to impress to get ahead.

In effect, you are most impressive when you bland in. That's right. I did not use the word blend. I purposely wrote that you should bland in. Blanding in makes it easier to get accepted by the key people who can make or break your career. In contrast, sticking out like a sore thumb makes it harder for decision makers to feel in sync or on the same wavelength with you.

Technique 3: Listen Attentively— It Makes a Powerful Impression

The third technique you can use to quickly make a great impression is to listen well.

The following tale illuminates the supreme importance of listening well:

A man decided he wanted to divorce his wife. They had been married for quite a few years. He went to a divorce lawyer. The lawyer asked him, "Have you ever loved your wife?"

The man replied, "Yes, I would have left her, but I was afraid to do that until now."

Then, the lawyer asked the man, "Why do you want to leave her?"

The man said, "Well, we have lots of trees around our house, but I always rake up all the leaves myself. She never helps with that."

The lawyer asked the man another question: "Has she been mean to you?"

The man answered, "I stopped eating red meat a few years ago. Now I eat only chicken or fish for protein."

Then, the lawyer posed this question, "Does she ever help around the house? For example, does she ever take out the garbage?"

To this, the man said, "We have a two-car garage."

The lawyer inquired, "Is it true that both of you jointly own a Ford?"

And the man replied, "We can afford whatever we want. Money is not a problem for us."

Finally, the man was getting frustrated, because he failed to understand the purpose of the lawyer's questions, so the man blurted, "You're the lawyer. Why don't you ask me some useful questions about my lousy marriage?"

So, the lawyer asked the man, "Why do you want to get divorced?"

And the man replied, "Because we can't communicate."

This story illustrates, perhaps in extreme fashion, the fact that many conversations or dialogues between two people actually are two monologues occurring simultaneously.

That happens because the participants often do not listen attentively to each other.

Please answer this question: How do you feel when someone does a poor job of listening to you? I asked numerous people this question. Most said they felt

* ignored
* unimportant
* offended
* frustrated

They often avoided spending much time or energy on anyone who failed to listen well to them.

While poor listening certainly produces resentment, attentive listening does the opposite. It

* creates comfort
* makes a good impression
* aids communication

Four Ways to Get the Most from What You Hear

Here are four techniques you can use to listen well:

1. Concentrate.
2. Paraphrase or repeat.
3. Ask questions.
4. Take notes.

First, you must *concentrate*. It is essential to pay attention to what a person says to you. All too often, instead of listening, we spend time figuring out what we want to say next. Sometimes we even think about totally unrelated matters. So, concentrate on what the other person says to you.

Second, *paraphrase* or *repeat* what the person said. When someone says something to you, you can say, "Let me see if I heard you correctly," and then repeat what the person said using the same or similar words. Make sure you heard it right.

Third, *ask questions*. You can say, "To help me make sure I have it right, please let me ask you a few questions." Then, ask questions to clarify or reinforce what you thought the person said.

The fourth listening tactic is the best but least used: *take notes*. Just carry paper and pen with you. To make sure you listened well, jot down notes as the person talks. Then, simply review the key details with the person. Ask the person to modify or clarify any points you wrote down.

You pick up a lot of useful information by using these four listening techniques. In addition, you generate a good impression, because people love when you listen to them. And you avoid the hazards created by poor listening skills; people don't feel ignored, unimportant, or frustrated.

WHAT ABOUT THE "REAL" YOU?

At this point, you may be wondering if I am telling you to "sell out" or be a phony. Perhaps you are a Results-Focused person, and I am saying that regardless of what you "naturally" are, if you are with a Friendly-Focused person, then you ought to behave in a Friendly-Focused fashion (or vice versa).

You might well be saying, "Mike, I understand your point, but that not the 'real' me."

But that is not all. I also suggested that you mirror body language, vocal style, and attire, regardless of how you "naturally" move, speak, or dress. I even advocated you listen well, even if you really do not want to.

All in all, you might be asking yourself, "Isn't this 'selling out'?"

Now, let me change the question. Let's put this "selling out" question in a different perspective. The French have a saying that goes like this:

> *A car could go just as far on square wheels*
> *as the car could go on round wheels. The*
> *difference is that on round wheels the ride*
> *is much, much smoother.*

Looked at from that perspective, my recommendations simply boil down to suggesting you go through life on round wheels—not square ones—and that if you do, you'll quickly make a great impression.

Picture someone you know who gets along with no one. This person has lots of rough edges and rubs many people the wrong way. If I could bet $1 million with you, I could probably safely bet that person acts the *same* way with just about everyone he or she meets—regardless of how the other person wants or likes to be treated. This person rides through life on square wheels—*not* on round wheels.

People who get along well with people alter their behavior slightly to meet the needs of each individual they meet. In sharp contrast, people who rub people the wrong way almost invariably act the same way with everyone.

Imagine a time you told a close friend some very personal, intimate details. If the next day you met somebody for the first time in your life, would you tell this new person the same personal, intimate details you told your close friend? Of course, you would never do that. However, no one would ever accuse you of "selling out," because it is not "selling out," is it? No, instead, people would say you *acted appropriately*.

People who get along well with other people behave a little differently with each human being they encounter so they can get along (at least to some degree) with each person. That is like going through life on round wheels, not square wheels. It is called "life," not "selling out."

Technique 4: Engage in Artful Vagueness— The Magic Way Out of a Sticky Situation

Although you want to make a good impression on others, you never want to contradict

* Your values
* What you know is right or wrong

To demonstrate how this fourth technique—to quickly make a great impression on practically any body—works, I will show you how to diplomatically handle sticky situations by describing one in which I found myself.

As mentioned earlier, I am an industrial psychologist. One aspect of my work entails developing preemployment tests that companies give to job candidates. My validated tests help companies do what I call "hire the best—and avoid the rest."[2] They use my tests to determine which applicants are most likely to be productive, dependable, and trustworthy if the company hires them.

One executive heard how my tests accurately predict who succeeds on the job. So he called, and asked me to meet with him and two of his colleagues.

At our meeting, I first listened to the problems they had in accurately evaluating candidates. In general, they had

---

[2]Readers interested in how companies use tests to pinpoint which job candidates may succeed on the job can read another book I wrote, entitled, *Hire the Best and Avoid the Rest*, N.Y., AMACOM, 1993.

hired too many employees who performed below expectations.

After listening, I told them how we could customize preemployment tests to help them pinpoint which job applicants were most likely to be productive, dependable, and honest on the job.

Unfortunately, these executives harbored misconceptions about preemployment tests. They described the testing program they wanted to start. It was a method that I knew from experience simply would not get them the results they wanted. It would not help them hire the best.

However, the more I explained how they were wrong, the more insistent they got that I should do it their way. Finally, I asked myself, "What's the matter here? I know they're wrong, but they keep arguing with me."

Suddenly, it dawned on me that I did not yet make them feel comfortable with me. The more I spoke against their proposal, the more uncomfortable they felt with me. They rightly noticed I was not on the same wavelength with them. We were not in sync.

Nevertheless, I definitely could not tell them they were right, since they were absolutely wrong. Instead, I sat back awhile, and intently listened again to their recommendations.

Then I said, "You know something? I've been listening very carefully to how you'd like to proceed on this project. And (here I paused for effect) *that's an idea.*"

At the same time, I thought to myself—but I did not say it out loud—"That's a *stupid* idea." However, I only said to them, "That's *an* idea."

What did they think? They probably interpreted "That's an idea" as me agreeing with them, or thinking they had a good idea. Did I say they had a good idea? Definitely not! I merely remarked, "That's *an* idea." Actually, *anything* anybody says is "an idea."

I used the fourth technique to quickly make a good impression on practically anyone. This technique is called *artful vagueness.*

I did this by falling back on the artfully vague phrase of "That's an idea."

I also could have used other artfully vague phrases, such as "You've got a point." Then, I could have thought to myself, "It's a *stupid* point." Would I have said that aloud? No. All I would have remarked is "You've got a point." The person hearing that probably would think I considered their point a *good* one. However, I would not have said that. By using artfully vague phrases, you could maintain or increase rapport and avoid 'selling out' to what you consider wrong.

Here is another artfully vague technique you can use. I learned this one from the managing partner of a major consulting firm. One day I visited his office. While we chatted, an executive from a client company called. The executive asked if the consulting firm ever did a specific type of consulting project this executive wanted done at his company.

This hot-shot consultant was probably the last person in the world who would even think of turning away any potential business. Although he knew his firm never did that exact type of consulting project, he figured his staff was resourceful and bright enough to figure out how to tackle it.

So, rather than saying "No" to this executive who was almost handing him consulting business, he listened very carefully to the request. The executive finally asked point blank, "Did your consulting firm ever handle a project like this?"

The consultant replied, "We most certainly have handled projects that are *to a degree* like it."

Realize this highly successful consultant used the artfully vague phrase "to a degree." This managing partner at a big consulting firm never said if "to a degree" meant 1 degree or 100 degrees. He just said, "to a degree." The executive who called him undoubtedly assumed that meant "Yes." As a result, the consulting firm landed that lucrative project.

How to Use Artful Vagueness to Defuse Anger

You also can use artful vagueness to get an angry person off your back. Picture the last time someone was really angry at you, and you argued back. That hostile person insisted you are a horrible-dumb-incompetent-unworthy-terrible humanoid. You defended yourself by asserting you are not bad and had good reason to do whatever provoked the other person's wrath. When you argued, that person probably got even more angry with you.

What could you do to defuse the torrents of anger? Use this technique that works wonders. Please remember that first you need to swallow your pride for five or ten minutes. Allow the person to vent loads of anger at you while you attentively listen.

Then, look the person in the eye, and say, "I listened very carefully to what you said to me and how you're so angry at me. And, you know something, *you may be right.*"

Did you say the person was right? Not at all. You merely acknowledged, "You *may* be right." You could think to yourself at the same time, "You may be wrong."

However, when you say "You may be right" to an angry person, the person starts feeling embarrassed. The hostile person gets the sense you gave in. But you did not. All you said was the person *"may* be right," not that he or she is right. This is often sufficient to make the angry person back off and stop venting anger at you.

Finally, there is another artfully vague technique you can use. Remember when your grandparents or some wise person told you that it is usually best not to talk about highly charged subjects, such as politics, money, and religion. They were right. Such touchy, personal topics easily (1) rub people the wrong way or (2) make them uncomfortable when they disagree with you.

Unfortunately, every once in awhile you run into people, who are important to your career or success, who never learned these rules. They insist you hear their views on politics, money, religion, or other sensitive matters. When this occurs, it is awkward to overtly disagree. The person then may not like you as much if you disagree or may withhold career opportunities you desire.

Here is how I handled such a sticky situation. One company wanted me to conduct many workshops for their employees. I met with the executive who contacted me. He started our meeting by telling me his political philosophy. His political philosophy, to put it nicely, reflected a fringe movement he belonged to and felt strongly about. Ninety-nine percent of the population would consider it bizarre and outrageous.

I most certainly disagreed with him. But this character kept rambling on, ranting and raving about his political philosophy.

Then, he directly asked me, "Well, what do you think of that?" What a sticky situation! I wanted to get his business, so I needed to avoid turning him off. However, I could not sell out my values and tell him I felt as he did. So, I looked him squarely in the eye, and told him totally truthfully, "You know something, I've been listening very carefully to your political philosophy, and I appreciate you explaining it so well to me. And I want you to know *that's something I think about very intensely at times.*"

I did not mention I think about it very intensely for just a few minutes annually—and only when it pops up in an article I read.

However, when he heard my artfully vague phrase— "It's something I think about very intensely at times"—he assumed it meant I agreed with him. That made him feel good and comfortable with me. At the same time, I *never* sold out, because I never told him I agreed with him. I simply said, "It's something I think about very intensely at times." Everyone thinks about things "at times." It never means we agree or disagree.

To summarize, you can use the following artfully vague phrases when you want to help a person feel comfortable with you, but want to avoid selling out your values or what you know is correct or incorrect:

* "That's an idea."
* "You've got a point."
* "...to a degree."
* "You may be right."
* "It's something I think about very intensely at times."

Technique 5: Use Everyone's Favorite Word— Their Name

Name calling is the fifth skill to help you quickly make a great impression. I recently gave a speech at a large convention. After the convention, I went to the airport to fly back to my hometown of Chicago. As I walked through the airport, I heard a very beautiful woman's voice loudly calling, "Michael, Michael, Michael!"

I instantly thought to myself, "That's a big compliment! It's probably someone who heard my speech at the convention and wants to talk with me. Maybe she bought one of my books, and wants me to autograph it."

So I turned around and there was the women who had yelled, "Michael, Michael, Michael!"

She was passionately kissing some guy whose name I must assume is Michael.

As this event illustrates, we all feel magnetized, drawn to, or mesmerized when we hear our name. That is why a person's name is his or her favorite word in the whole world. Other data on this phenomenon came out when I tagged along with high-achievers and underachievers at their jobs. I observed an intriguing use of name calling. With few exceptions, high-achievers used the name of the person they spoke to at least once in each conversation. In contrast, underachievers used the name of the person they encountered less than half the time.

This means high-achievers tend to use the name of the people they talk with *much* more than underachievers. Name calling is a wonderfully easy, valuable tactic everyone can use every day.

Technique 6: Pay Three Compliments a Day

While following around many high-achievers and under-achievers for my research, I noticed an amazing difference. The high-achievers—the winners—paid an average of *three compliments per day*. The underachievers—people who are equally intelligent but just doing average or even below average in their careers—seldom gave compliments.

This provides a vital key to success with people. When you give someone a *sincere* compliment, it makes the person receiving the compliment feel special. It also raises his or her opinion of you. And, as if that were not enough, giving a compliment

* requires only a few seconds of your valuable time
* costs you nothing
* makes you feel good while you helped the other person feel good

And you reap even more benefits when you dispense sincere compliments. Giving a person a compliment proves the wisdom of the phrase, "What goes around comes around." When you give someone a compliment and then a day later or a week later or even a year later you need to persuade the person to do something, the person will recall the compliment, which made him feel fabulous, and that will make him easier to persuade.

Isn't that great? You earned all those benefits by paying a compliment that took you a few seconds to give, did not cost you anything, and made you feel good as you said it to the person.

To summarize, always remember the principle of making a great impression:

Human beings want to be around people
who seem similar to themselves.

To accomplish this, you need to work to *help people feel comfortable with you.* That is, help people feel you

* are in sync with them
* are on their same wavelength
* understand their thoughts, needs, feelings, and opinions

This chapter described a half dozen ways to develop such rapport. You can use the following checklist to improve your ability to help make people feel comfortable with you and create a good impression.

CHECKLIST—
HOW TO MAKE A GREAT IMPRESSION

_____ Recognize the 4 Interpersonal Styles
  _____ Results-focused
  _____ Detail-focused
  _____ Friendly-focused
  _____ Partying-focused
_____ Mirror
  _____ Body language
  _____ Vocal style
  _____ Attire
_____ Listen attentively
  _____ Concentrate
  _____ Paraphrase or repeat
  _____ Ask questions
  _____ Take notes
_____ Engage in artful vagueness
  _____ "That's an idea."
  _____ "You've got a point."
  _____ ". . . to a degree."
  _____ "You may be right."
  _____ "It's something I think about very intensely at times."
_____ Use people's names
_____ Give three sincere compliments each day

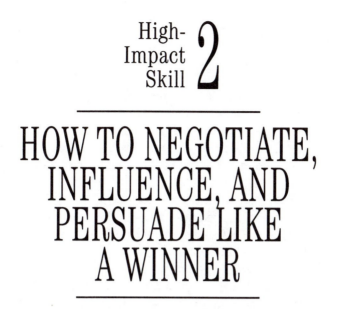

High-
Impact
Skill 2

HOW TO NEGOTIATE, INFLUENCE, AND PERSUADE LIKE A WINNER

My research shows the second most important people skill used by high-achievers is their ability to smoothly and diplomatically persuade, influence, and negotiate. In this chapter, I will use those three terms interchangeably.

WIN-WIN: THE BEST POSSIBLE RESULT

Every time you work to influence someone, remember only three possible outcomes may result from a negotiating situation:

1. Lose-lose
2. Win-lose
3. Win-win

The first possible outcome, *lose-lose* occurs when both you and the other person end up worse off than before you started negotiating. Both of you lost something. Since no wise person wants that situation, we will focus on how to avoid lose-lose outcomes.

A second possible outcome is a *win-lose* ending to the negotiation. That happens when one negotiator "puts something over" on the other person. At this point, you may think to yourself, "Arriving at a win-lose outcome would be fine with me—as long as I'm the one who wins and the other person loses."

However, such things are not always what they appear to be, and could get you into a mess. The loser may not take the loss lying down. He may conjure up some way, sooner or later, to get back at you.

For example, if you work for a company, the next time that person deals with your organization he may try to make trouble for you. He might feel that since you made him lose last time, this time he can win at the expense of you or someone else in your company. Given the possible negative repercussions from win-lose outcomes, you definitely want to avoid such results.

The third possible outcome is a *win-win* outcome. That's where you and the other person both wind up better off as a result of the negotiation. Perhaps you did not get everything you wanted, and the other person may not have gotten everything he or she wanted. However, in the end, both of you are somewhat better off than before you started negotiating.

2-Step Negotiating Method

Much of negotiating boils down to using a two-step technique called the "pace-and-then-lead" technique. Specifically,

Step 1. Pace.

Step 2. Lead.

These terms are used in neurolinguistic programming, a communications skills system.

Pacing is the first step; leading is the second. What does it mean to pace and lead? To pace means you help someone feel

* comfortable with you
* on the same wavelength
* in sync

Or, at the very least, you leave the person with the sense that you understand his or her

* Thoughts
* Needs
* Feelings
* Opinions

Pacing should prove fairly easy for you since, in the last chapter, you discovered how to make a great impression on practically anyone. All the techniques described in that chapter are pacing techniques, and those same techniques are used in the first step of negotiating.

Pacing forms the foundation of negotiating. Just as you would not build a house without first laying the foundation, you also will find it easier to *successfully* persuade someone if you first pace the person.

After you pace someone so he feels comfortable with you, then proceed to the second step of negotiating. This is called "leading." That's when you work on leading—or convincing or swaying or influencing—the other person to use your ideas, services, or products.

This chapter focuses quite a bit on the pace-and-then-lead technique. Now, let us work on applying an array of persuasion skills.

3 WINNING PERSUASION SKILLS

Persuasion Skill 1:
Ask for What You Want

The first leading skill is *asking*. This is the most elementary persuasion technique, and often could be the first one for you to use. However, many people feel too embarrassed to ask for what they want and, therefore, skip one of the simplest negotiating tactics ever created.

This is a true story: Only one person in the world ever organized and produced an immense, international ballet extravaganza like the one I will describe to you. This person lives in Chicago, and this magnificent event took place in Chicago.

The event's organizer arranged for about a dozen of the world's most outstanding ballet dancers and ballet companies to appear in a spectacular week-long event. No one in the ballet world ever succeeded in pulling off such an amazing feat.

When I asked the organizer, "How did you manage to arrange for all these world-class stars and highly acclaimed companies to appear in one city during the same week?" she looked at me rather puzzled, and replied, "All I did was *ask* them." That may not seem like much, but then again few people ever think just to ask for what they want.

So, the first and most basic negotiating technique boils down to just asking for what you want. If that does not succeed, then you can use more sophisticated techniques.

Persuasion Skill 2:
Adopt the Pace-and-Then-Lead Technique

A slightly more complicated persuasion skill is the *"pace-and-then-lead" technique*. To use this, first you make a pace statement, and then you follow it with a lead. That is, first you pace to help the person feel comfortable with you and then you lead.

Here is a situation using the simple pace-and-then-lead technique.

Imagine you are speaking with someone whom you want to convince to work on a project with you. This person just mentioned an idea that might be useful for the project. You could remark, "Your idea is good, *and* it should be plugged into the project that I need your help to complete."

Let's dissect this statement. It uses the pace-and-then-lead technique, as follows:

* ✳ Pace: "Your idea is good"

* ✳ Lead: "...and it should be plugged into the project that I need your help to complete."

How would you feel toward someone who told you, "Your idea is good." Most people would feel pretty comfortable with that person. After all, anyone who agrees with you probably is fairly bright and certainly makes you feel good!

Important Note: When you use the pace-and-then-lead technique, always connect the two statements with the word "*and*." Avoid using the words "but" or "however."

Think about the last time someone said something to you, and then popped in the word "but" or "however." For instance, the person may have said to you, "Your idea is good, *but*..." or "You have an interesting way to do that, *however*...." Regardless of the wonderful pace or compliment ("Your idea is good") said first, after you heard the word "but," you probably thought that person would verbally slap your face. As soon as you heard the words "but" or "however," you realized a hitch existed. And that was not what you wanted, was it?

You may have noticed good salespeople tend to use the word "and." They *purposely* rarely say "but" or "however." Reason: Their success rests on keeping comfort and rapport with people they need to influence. Words like "but" or "however" make the person on the receiving end cringe and feel uncomfortable and uptight. That throws a wrench into any attempt to influence them.

Persuasion Skill 3:
Ask the "Right" Questions

The third technique is using questions properly. You might think to yourself, "How could I persuade somebody by using questions?" There definitely are ways you can do that. Let me describe them to you.

Gerard Nierenberg, author of *The Art of Negotiating*, pointed out that questions reveal how a person thinks. Nierenberg also asserted that properly asked questions uncover the other side's needs during a negotiation. Using questions helps you find out the other person's

* Thoughts
* Needs
* Feelings
* Opinions
* Desires
* Goals

Those are make-it-or-break-it bits of information. After all, when you understand what is going on inside a person's brain, you find it a lot easier to figure out how to persuade, influence, and negotiate with that person.

Only two types of questions exist in the entire world. These are

* Closed-ended questions
* Open-ended questions

A closed-ended question requires a person to answer mainly by saying yes or no, this or that, *or* "X" or "Y." The person does not need to think much nor talk much to explain his or her thoughts, needs, feelings, opinions, desires, and goals.

In sharp contrast to closed-ended questions are open-ended questions. When you ask people an open-ended question, they most certainly cannot just answer "yes" or "no," "this or that," or "X" or "Y." Instead, when you ask an open-ended question, the person must

* Think about the question
* Explain his or her thoughts, needs, feelings, opinions, desires, and goals

Examine the sample closed-ended and open-ended questions shown on page 60. The closed-ended question, "Do you like your new job?" just begs for someone to answer only, "Yes, I like my new job" or "No, I don't."

Let's rephrase that into an open-ended question. Instead of asking, "Do you like your new job?", the open-ended approach would be, "Tell me about your new job." Now, the person cannot answer just "yes" or "no." His answer can venture off into hundreds of different directions.

Closed-Ended Versus Open-Ended Questions

Closed-Ended	*Open-Ended*
"Do you like your new job?"	"Tell me about your new job."
"Would you help me do this project?"	"What are your ideas for how to finish this project quickly?"
"Can you deliver this equipment by the last day of this month?"	"What will you do to make sure the equipment is delivered by the last day of the month?"

He can tell you how he loves or hates his job. He could describe his boss, colleagues, work schedule, travel schedule, or the working conditions. This open-ended inquiry does not lock him into saying just "yes" or "no." By asking an open-ended question, you can discover crucial details about a person's thoughts, needs, feelings, opinions, desires, and goals.

Here is another closed-ended question: "Would you help me do this project?" That begs for a "yes" or "no" answer. However, when you ask people to help on a project, you yearn for them to say "yes." So, if you ask this closed-ended question, "Would you help me do this project?", you have only a 50-50 chance of getting your desired "yes" answer.

You can use an open-ended question to get the person thinking and talking and, perhaps, convincing himself that he may want to work with you on this project.

To do that, instead of asking the closed-ended question, "Would you help me do this project?" you could ask, "What are your ideas for how to finish this project quickly?"

Suddenly, when you ask that question the person needs to think and talk more to you. And—as anyone who ever motivated another person knows—the more someone comes up with an idea for how to work on a project, the more motivated that person may feel about actually working on the project.

In fact, one of the worst actions a manager can take is to tell an employee precisely what to do. Instead, it works better to ask an open-ended question that encourages the person to (1) think about what to do and (2) tell you her ideas or opinions about how to handle the project. Furthermore, when an employee does such thinking and explaining, the employee may end up talking himself into working on the project.

Let's examine a third example of a closed-ended question and its open-ended alternative. The closed-ended question may be to ask an equipment salesperson, "Can you deliver the equipment by the last day of this month?"

The salesperson can answer "yes" or "no." By asking that question, you most likely want the equipment delivered by the last day of the month. Unfortunately, with a closed-ended question, you have a 50% chance of hearing "no."

Fortunately, an open-ended alternative exists: "What will you do to make sure you deliver the equipment by the last day of the month?" This open-ended question accomplishes two goals. First, it is open-ended, so the salesperson cannot just say "no" to you. Second, embedded in this question is the assumption that the person definitely will deliver the equipment by the last day of the month or before. Your open-ended question merely helps the person pinpoint how to do it.

Actually, it is easy to ask open-ended questions and avoid asking closed-ended questions. Simply start the questions using the words such as those shown in column 2 and avoid those in column 1.

Words Starting Closed-Ended Questions	*Words Starting Open-Ended Questions*
"Do you...?"	"What...?"
"Can you...?"	"How...?"
"Will you...?"	"Tell me...."
"Is...?"	"Describe...."
"Was...?"	

Interestingly, in certain workshops I have the participants practice asking both closed-ended and open-ended questions. Their reactions to the two types of questions are remarkably different. Participants say that asking closed-ended questions was quick. All they got were "yes" or "no" answers. But they also uncovered minimal information. Closed-ended questions overwhelmingly focus on the needs of the person asking the question and do not expose the thoughts, needs, feelings, or opinions of the person asked the closed-ended question.

Also, when you ask a lot of closed-ended questions, you typically spend a lot of time and energy conjuring up your next question while the other person is answering you. That leaves you with barely any time to listen to the person's answers!

In contrast, open-ended questions help you acquire more knowledge about the other person's thoughts, needs, feelings, opinions, desires, and goals. And, as I mentioned before, that crucial information helps you persuade, influence, and negotiate. The more you know about the other person's interests and motivations, the more easily and successfully you can influence the person. Also, the personal disclosures stimulated by open-ended questions help you and the other person feel emotionally closer. That helps you pace the person.

I notice everyone's favorite topic is talking about themselves—their thoughts, needs, feelings, and opinions. The more you get people to self-disclose, the more

* comfortable they feel with you
* they like you

Such feelings pave the way to successfully persuading, influencing, and negotiating.

HOW TO GET PEOPLE INTO THE HABIT OF AGREEING WITH YOU

Despite the bad rap I have just given to closed-ended questions, they do serve some useful purposes. For instance, imagine you are in a room with me. You stand or sit at the back of a room, and I am at the front. Now, imagine you would like me to walk from the front of the room to the back of the room.

We could play a game. In our game, you ask me questions. Every time you ask me a question and I answer "yes," I move one step toward the back of the room. Each time you ask a question to which I respond "no," I move a step away from you.

If you want me to walk from the front of the room to the back of the room, your best strategy is to continually ask me questions to which I reply "yes." You must avoid asking questions that lead me to responding "no."

You easily can accomplish that by using "yes-able" questions. These are closed-ended questions to which people are bound to answer "yes" 99.9 % of the time. The more you get someone to agree—say "yes"—to you, the more likely it is that the person will get into the *habit* of going along with what you want.

For instance, think about somebody you know who you always agree with. You got into the habit of almost always saying "yes." In all likelihood, when that person wants to persuade you to do something, before that person even finishes asking you to do it, you already decided you will do it.

You probably know someone with whom you usually disagree. This person typically hears you say "no." If you are like most people, when that person starts asking you to do something—even before he or she finishes asking you—you probably already are cooking up reasons to say "no" and refuse that person's request.

These familiar tendencies point out how crucial it is to get people you want to persuade into the *habit* of saying "yes" to you. That eases and speeds up your persuasion task. The opposite is also true. The more someone habitually says "no" to you, or disagrees with you, the less likely it is that you can successfully persuade that person.

A good way to ask "yes-able" questions is to ask something you know the person will agree with. If you want, you also can add phrases to the question, such as

* ❋ "Isn't it?"

* ❋ "Right?"

* ❋ "Don't you agree?"

For example, a salesperson could ask this yes-able question to a prospect: "The cost of the equipment you want to buy is important, *isn't it?*" Ninety-nine percent of the time the price *is* important. So, such a question surely would yield a "yes" answer, and perhaps begin the process of getting the prospect into the habit of saying "yes" to the salesperson.[1]

---

[1]Once when I used this example in a negotiating workshop I was presenting at a company, the company's vice president of finance was sitting in the front row. When I mentioned this question, she turned around and announced to everyone in the room, "If any of you ever answers 'no' to that question, you're fired!"

Or, the same salesperson could ask a potential customer, "Isn't the cost of the equipment important to you?" Again, that is a yes-able closed-ended question. Just about everyone would answer "yes" to it.

When an employee wants to prompt a co-worker to start working on a project, the employee could ask this "yes-able" question, "We need to finish this project pretty soon, don't we?" Here, a true statement—"We need to finish this project pretty soon"—is followed by a "yes-able" question—"don't we?"—that begs for a "yes" reply.

This "yes-able" technique could prove helpful at times. *Right?* You probably caught on to how to do it, *didn't you?* Now, you have one more tool to use to help people get into the habit of agreeing with you, *don't you?*

HOW TO USE THE "OR" TECHNIQUE TO GET ACTION

Another tactic that gets people to go along with you is the "Or" technique. Let's look at an example. Remember a time you spoke to someone on the phone and it seemed apparent that you and the other person should talk face to face. So, you remarked, "It seems like it would be good for us to get together."

And this person replied, "Yes. Well, um, ah, um, give me a call next week [or next month or next decade]." Since you were not born yesterday, you quickly realize this really meant you should contact the person again during the next decade. This person wished to avoid meeting with you.

Here is a solution that works really well. I use it all the time, because it helps me land appointments that I otherwise would not get. Use the "Or" technique to land appointments with people who feel less than exuberant about meeting with you. For instance, you might remark, "It seems like we should get together, shouldn't we?" (By the way, that's a yes-able, closed-ended question, isn't it?) If you built up to this correctly, the person would say, "Yes."

Then, you could comment, "Well, I'll be near your office next week, probably Thursday *or* Friday. Which day would be better to get together—Thursday *or* Friday?" The person might answer, "Friday is better."

Then you could say, "Great. We can get together on Friday."

Then, ask, "Which would be better for you, morning *or* afternoon?" The person might say afternoon.

You say, "O.K. What time would you like to get together in the afternoon—1 P.M. *or* 2 P.M.?" The person might say 2 P.M. Finally, you would summarize your agreement by saying, "I'll look forward to getting together with you Friday afternoon at 2 P.M."

What did you do? You gave the person two choices with the word "*or*" in between the choices. You easily could live with either of the two choices. You merely inserted "*or*" so the person you want to influence can make the final decision. For example, you asked the person,

* "Thursday *or* Friday?"
* "Morning *or* afternoon?"
* "1 P.M. *or* 2 P.M.?"

Each time, you let the other person make the final choice. The "Or" technique works especially well when you want to get people to choose some action.

2-STEP METHOD TO OVERCOME RESISTANCE

To persuade, influence, or negotiate successfully, you must know how to handle a problem that undoubtedly will pop up. Specifically, despite your good intentions, some people will resist your ideas or proposals—no matter how brilliant they are. They will erect barricades to block your propositions.

How do you feel inside when someone objects to or resists your ideas? I've asked that to many people. They say it most certainly throws up a roadblock to influencing the person. They often respond by feeling

* defensive

* angry

* disappointed

* sorry they even made the suggestion

These typical emotional reactions bubble up inside people when someone objects to or resists their suggestions.

Regardless, a simple 2-step technique exists that helps you overcome objections or resistance. It is the pace-and-then-lead technique that we looked at earlier. First you pace, and then you lead.

To understand why this two-step tactic works, ask yourself, "What is it that people really are telling me between the lines when they object, resist or toss a roadblock in front of my fantastic idea?"

Between the lines, they really are saying,

* "I don't feel comfortable with you."

* "I sense we're not on the same wavelength."

* "We are not in sync."

* "You don't understand my thoughts, needs, feelings, and opinions."

The vital question is: "What do you do right away to help make someone feel...

* comfortable?"

❋ in sync with you?"

❋ on the same wave length?"

❋ understood?"

You ought to answer that you pace them. You use the techniques revealed earlier to make a great impression.

The next time someone disagrees with your clever notions, try pacing him with

❋ *Active listening and paraphrase.* For example, you could say, "Let me see if I understand your objection. You object to such-and-such...."

❋ *Agreement.* Say, "You know something, you've got a *good* point. I agree with you. That is a problem with my recommendation."

❋ *An artfully vague phrase.* If the person plainly is wrong or does not understand your proposition, you could say, "You know, I've been listening to your objection, and you've got a point" or "That's an idea" or "You may be right."

After you regain rapport with the person, proceed on to leading. This could include

❋ Asking for what you want

❋ Using open-ended questions

❋ Using "yes-able" and "Or" closed-ended questions

For instance, ask the person how you might proceed with your proposal to make her feel more comfortable with it.

Here is an example of how this works. Let's say you want someone to work on a project with you. However, she objects by saying, "I'm too busy to work on that project."

You can't respond, "Who cares how busy you are? Do it anyway." That may be what you would like to say. However, to put it mildly, it would rub the person the wrong way.

Remember:

When people object to your ideas, what they really are saying is that they do not feel comfortable with you. They want you to do something or say something to make them feel comfortable.

So, you could pace her by saying, "I know you're very busy." That pace will help her feel you understand her concerns.

Then, you could lead by asking this open-ended question: "How can we reschedule your tasks so you'll have enough time to work on this project?" This question would prompt her to think and plan how she could work on the project.

Keep in mind that

* When you are doing well at persuading someone, just keep leading.

* The moment the person objects to your suggestions or ideas, *immediately* start pacing.

Use pacing tactics to help the other person feel you are on the same wavelength or that you at least understand his thoughts, needs, feelings, opinions, desires, and goals.

ONE WORD WINNERS SHOULD NEVER USE

A word exists that you should avoid like a plague. Never use this one word!

To help make my point, I will ask you some questions that I would like you to answer as you read them. Name something that you consider really important in your life. (Come up with something.)

Why do you consider that important?

Why is that so important to you?

Why do you focus your energy on that?

Why do you think that's a big deal?

Why do you think that's special?

If someone posed such "why?" questions to you, two alarms would go off in your head. First, you probably started feeling pushed "up against the wall," so to speak. Second, you most likely felt uncomfortable having to justify your answers.

In general, when you ask someone a question with the word "why," in effect you are questioning whether or not the person has the brain power to clearly and intelligently think through a situation. Using "why" in a question implies you suspect the person had outpatient brain surgery—and the scalpel slipped.

Therefore, simply *avoid using the word "why."* It all too easily leaves people feeling uncomfortable with you.

If you really want to know why, you could ask,

* "How did you happen to come up with that?"

* "What led you to that conclusion?"

* "How did you arrive at that solution?"

These are kinder ways to ask why. So, abstain from using the word "why" and use these other phrases, instead.

MORE SUREFIRE NEGOTIATING TECHNIQUES

Let's look at a number of additional negotiating techniques. As we move from one to the next, I strongly urge you to think about how you could use each technique in specific situations you were in or will face in your

* Personal life
* Career

Then, as you enter situations in which you must influence others, you can pick and choose from this smorgasbord of tactics to help you arrange win-win outcomes.

Robin Hood Technique

You probably did not realize Robin Hood was a commodity trader. Robin Hood and his band of merry men roamed the countryside in England. While doing this, they bought lambs or sheep from farmers. At that time, lambs were only eaten by the peasants. The rich did not eat such "lowly peasant food."

Since only poor folks ate sheep, Robin Hood and his band of merry men could buy the lambs or sheep very cheaply. They, then, took the sheep, which they would butcher, to the wealthy sections of the villages. They would sell the lamb meat to the rich villagers. Of course, Robin Hood did not tell them they were buying sheep. Instead, they would market the meat as venison, that is, deer meat. Since rich people highly valued venison, they would pay high prices for the meat. As a result, Robin Hood made huge profits.

By pulling off such deals, Robin Hood became a commodity trader. Reason: He would buy sheep and sell deer.

Or, in negotiating terms, Robin Hood would buy cheap and sell dear. Sometimes we now phrase it as *buy low and sell high.*

Kidding and cheating aside, buying low and selling high typically offers the best way to bargain. Just follow these easy-to-remember routines:

* When selling something, ask for more than you expect to get.
* When buying something, offer less than the asking price.

For example, perhaps you want to buy a car, and you are willing to spend $20,000. Would you even consider telling the salesperson you are willing to spend $20,000? Of course not. If you did, the salesperson would figure $20,000 is your lowest bid, and you would pay more.

Instead you might say, "I'm willing to spend $17,000 on the car." Then, you have leeway to get negotiated up to $20,000.

Now, let's put you in the salesperson's role. A prospect approaches you and asks, "How much is that car?" Perhaps as the salesperson you really want to get $20,000 for it. However, if you say $20,000, what would the buyer think? The buyer would presume, "Aha!! $20,000 is the high point of the car's price range. I can negotiate downward from $20,000."

Realizing this may occur, as the salesperson you may say, "The car costs $23,000." That leaves you room to negotiate downward, maybe down to about $20,000, nab the sale, and help your customer feel he or she landed a good deal on the "$23,000" car.

As a guideline, whenever possible, aim to

* Bid low when you are the buyer

❋ Ask for a higher amount if you are the seller

or just, remember the axiom of *buy low and sell high.*
You also can use the buy-low-and-sell-high approach in organizations. Let's say you want someone to collaborate with you on *one* project. If you believe the person will object quite strenuously, simply ask the person to cooperate with you on *two* projects.

Then, let the person negotiate out of her involvement in one of the two projects. By doing this, you accomplish two things. First, the other person feels she won, because she negotiated her way out of doing one of the two projects. Second, you got what you wanted: She agreed to work on *one* project. Using this buy-low-and-sell-high method produced a result that felt like a win-win to both parties.

I used a variation of this when I bought a television set. I found a store with a reasonable price for the TV I wanted. Then, I told the salesperson that I wanted both (1) a *free* service contract and (2) *free* service in my home if the TV needed repair. The salesperson told me, as I already knew, that the store "always" charged for *both* the contract and in-home service.

As I began to *slowly* put my credit card back into my wallet (to show my earnestness), I told the salesperson I would not buy the television if the store would not budge. Lo and behold, the salesperson offered me a free multiyear service contract and house calls for only $20 maximum (below the regular charge). I bought the television. By asking for *two* items and negotiating down to the *one* I most wanted, I felt it was a win. And the salesperson who could write up the order also got a win.

Another use of buy-low-and-sell-high could occur when someone asks you to manage a project. If you do not want to manage the project, you might propose working on part of the project but not take charge of the entire project.

This situation illustrates how to start negotiating by offering less than what you feel willing to do. Then, allow the other person to bargain you up a bit. This provides another opportunity for you to benefit from the buy-low-sell-high technique.

Time Is on Your Side

I call the second negotiating tactic *Time Is on Your Side*. During a workshop I conduct on how to negotiate, influence, and persuade, workshop participants practice negotiating in a number of situations. One involves pairing each participant with another. I give each person a sheet of information about the situation to be negotiated.

Importantly, each sheet gives different information about the situation. Then, I tell the participants they

* have *exactly* 5 minutes to negotiate
* *must* reach a win-win outcome

Lo and behold, it typically takes workshop participants about 4 minutes and 59 seconds to negotiate a win-win outcome.

This result demonstrates a fascinating phenomenon. Sometimes, instead of saying that people have 5 minutes to negotiate a win-win outcome, I tell them they have 15 minutes. Question: How long does it take most participants to reach a win-win outcome? Answer: Typically, about 14 minutes and 59 seconds.

I have also told people that they have one-half hour. I bet you can predict what occurred. It then takes about 29 minutes and 59 seconds for them to reach a win-win outcome.

In fact, I once gave workshop participants the exact same scenario, and told them they could take up to 45 minutes to negotiate win-win outcomes. You definitely can predict how long it took. It took them between 44 and 45 minutes to reach win-win outcomes.

As the old truism indicates, "*Work expands to take up the time.*" Likewise, remember when you negotiate that "time (in this case establishing a deadline) is on your side."

The general manager of a large store attended one of my negotiating workshops. After I discussed the "Time Is on Your Side" technique, she said,

"Mike, that's so true. When we advertise a 'special sale,' we often say the sale starts Friday and ends at 5 P.M. on Sunday. Often, on Friday and Saturday you can shoot a cannon through the middle of the store and not hit anybody. But on Sunday, starting about 4 o'clock—about an hour before we end the sale—customers pack into the store to take advantage of it."

This anecdote shows how work—and negotiating—definitely does expand to take up the allotted time. When you give people a reasonable time limit to wrap up negotiations, they typically use all or most of that time, but do come to a decision or complete the task. For example, if you negotiate with somebody to finish a project by Friday at 5 P.M., the person will most likely hand it to you between 4 and 5 o'clock. People often wait until the last minute. So you can make sure people do things on time by giving them a definite, but reasonable, time limit.

This explains why we often hear threats made during union contract negotiations: "Unless we sign a contract by midnight on Tuesday, we'll go on strike." When does the contract negotiation usually conclude? Usually by 11:59 P.M.! If a union says it needs to agree on a contract by 4 A.M. on Wednesday morning, probably the same contract clauses would be agreed on by 3:59 A.M. on Wednesday morning.

So set reasonable time limits when you negotiate.

Brainstorming

A third negotiating tactic is *brainstorming*. This works well when

* ❈ the negotiation seems friendly
* ❈ both sides want to come up with creative solutions

You could say to the people you are negotiating with, "Let's brainstorm. Let's conjure up creative, innovative alternatives or options."

Follow through by encouraging everyone to come up with ideas as you write them all on a flip chart. Warning: Don't let anyone criticize anyone else's ideas while brainstorming. Reason: Remember the last time you came up with an array of creative ideas—and someone criticized them. What happened to your level of creativity? It probably dropped to rock bottom. Why? Because when people are criticized as they come up with ideas, their creativity level shrinks. They become self-conscious.

For brainstorming to be effective, use a 2-step technique. First, ask people in the group to come up with creative solutions and write them all down, regardless of how outlandish or stupid or crazy or wild the idea seems. Second, when you finish brainstorming, decide as a group which innovative, creative solutions or alternatives could best overcome the problem or resolve the situation.

Tip: When you lead the brainstorming session during your negotiation, ask lots of open-ended questions to elicit creative ideas. Open-ended questions prod people to think about potential alternatives.

Tom Sawyer

The next negotiating technique is the *Tom Sawyer* technique. Here is how this negotiating tactic got its name.

A newspaper company needed to fill the publisher/chief operating officer position in its largest circulation newspaper. The job paid about $150,000 per year, plus up to 50% bonus money if the paper achieved specific profit goals.

The newspaper company finally narrowed its search down to two candidates. Both were experienced publishers of other newspapers. I interviewed and tested one candidate in the morning and the second candidate in the afternoon. Both candidates were asked many of the same questions. One question was, "What was your favorite childhood story and how did it go?"

The successful candidate replied, "My favorite childhood story was *Tom Sawyer*. It's about a boy who has to paint a fence but he just doesn't want to. So, he finds a few kids, and he shows them how much fun it can be to paint a fence. Then, the kids paint the fence and have a lot of fun doing it. Meanwhile, Tom does things he enjoys doing, and everyone is smiling because everyone is doing what he finds fun to do."

This incident led me to "discover" the Tom Sawyer negotiating approach. When you want to persuade someone to work on a project, find a facet of the project the person would enjoy doing. People are always more motivated doing something they enjoy than something they don't enjoy. *Tom Sawyer had the right idea.*

Fait Accompli *Approach*

The next negotiating technique is *"Fait Accompli."* In French, *fait accompli* means accomplished fact, a "done deal." It is "a given" or something that definitely will occur. The *fait accompli* persuasion technique quickly gets someone to do what you want him to do.

How? By stating what you want done and when you want it as though it were "a given" or a *fait accompli*. If you do this right, you should get what you want.

For example, let's say you want someone to finish a project and it needs to be finished by the tenth of the month. You can say to that person, "Here's a project we need you to complete by the tenth of the month. What are your ideas for how you can complete it by then?" Notice that embedded in the first part of this statement—"Here's a project we need you to complete by the tenth of the month"—is the phrase clearly implying the person *will* complete the project by the tenth of the month. After that *fait accompli* statement, you just need to ask an open-ended question—"What are your ideas for how you can complete it by then?"—to help him conjure up how he will complete the project by the tenth of the month.

Warning: You might use *fait accompli* with somebody one, two, or three times annually. However, if you do it more often, many people will object. Or consider it a win-lose proposition. So, use *fait accompli* when you *absolutely* need something done *and* less assertive methods fall on deaf ears.

The "Higher Authority" Technique

This technique enables you to get out of a negotiation session diplomatically when you cannot maneuver the other side into focusing on anything but a win-lose or lose-lose outcome. Using the *"Higher Authority"* tactic helps you save face as you slip out of the negotiating session.

To use this method, you could declare, "Before I can commit any effort to that project, I need to get my boss's o.k. Unfortunately, she's out of town until next month."

Such a statement conveys that before you can reach a final solution, you need to talk to somebody who just happens *not* to be readily available. When you invoke the "Higher Authority" technique, be certain the person with whom you claim you must speak won't stroll into the room minutes later.

Here's another "Higher Authority" gambit you can use. You might say to a salesperson, "I can't agree on the price you want until I talk to my boss–partner–spouse–colleagues–co-workers." Again, the gist is the same: You claim you absolutely must talk with somebody who

✻ Just happens not to be there

✻ Is hard to reach

This tactic lets you exit a lose-lose or win-lose situation and gives you time to modify your approach and return with a negotiating strategy that, hopefully, generates a win-win outcome.

The Back Burner Tactic

The *Back Burner* routine helps you avoid discussing a topic you prefer not to negotiate at that particular moment. When you negotiate, you usually want to negotiate topics *you* consider most important first. Once negotiations on those issues are completed, you may be willing to negotiate or discuss other topics.

One way to do this is to say, "Let's put that topic on the back burner until we agree on these other issues" to someone who raises a topic in the middle of a negotiating session that you prefer not to discuss. By the way, "these other issues" might be those points you want to discuss.

Here's another way to employ the Back Burner technique. When your counterpart tries to bring up another topic, you could say, "Yes, that's an important topic for us to deal with, and let's do it. First, let's tackle the matters currently on our agenda." Those matters happen to be the topics you consider most important.

The FBI Technique

Never use this negotiating technique with anyone

* ❋ who works in your organization
* ❋ with whom you want to have a warm relationship

It can easily foster a win-lose or lose-lose outcome, unless you do it right. This technique uses power negotiating and is called the *FBI* technique.

In an FBI-type interrogation, two investigators grill one person. One investigator acts nice, friendly, and warm. The other acts bad, mean, and vicious. Put another way, one interrogator acts like a "good parent," while the other one acts like a "bad parent."

What happens is that the person being questioned—or, in our case, negotiated with—is eager to do almost anything to get the attention of the investigator who seems nice *and* to avoid confronting the mean questioner.

When should you use the FBI negotiating ploy? Never with people you work with. Use it with vendors or salespeople to help you negotiate price concessions.

When I present the FBI technique in my negotiating workshop, some participants ask if it automatically sets up a win-lose outcome. If done improperly, it could. However, keep in mind the reason you have chosen this technique: You do it to win price concessions from a vendor or salesperson. The salesperson entered the negotiation with one *primary goal*: To sell you something. Your *primary goal* is to get the best price. Therefore, if the salesperson makes a sale *and* you get a better price, both of you achieved your primary goals. That definitely sounds like a win-win outcome.

The Ultimatum

The next negotiating technique is *Ultimatums*. Sometimes people misunderstand this. I said earlier we need to aim for win-win outcomes, and we can arrive at win-win outcomes with the types of ultimatums described here. However, this is an aggressive negotiating strategy.

Ultimatums can prove useful when you want to

* make the other side give in
* call your opponent's bluff

You have to be careful that when you present an ultimatum, you follow through. You can't back down without losing face or getting a bad reputation.

For example, with a salesperson, you might use this ultimatum: "Either sell us the equipment for $10,000 less, or you can forget about selling it to us at all."

Here's another way you can use an ultimatum. You might say, "If you do not accept this agreement, then we'll need to call off even trying to reach an agreement."

For example, a boss may say to her subordinate, "Either you agree to improve your job performance in the four ways we discussed, or I will have to let you go." That is a clear ultimatum. If the employee wants his job, then this ultimatum—while tense—could result in a win-win outcome.

The major problem negotiators create for themselves with ultimatums is they fail to follow through. Remember: Prior to giving someone an ultimatum, ask yourself, "Can I live with it?" If, for instance, you make a "final offer" and the other side does not take it, you are obligated (unless you're willing to lose face) to call off *any* possible deal. So before making an ultimatum, you must make sure you can get the services or products from someone else. Otherwise, you could be "up the creek without a paddle."

Vanish: An Ideal Technique When Only You Can Make the Deal

When used properly, the *Vanish* technique forces the other side in a negotiation to run after you before a final agreement can be reached. Warning: Use Vanish only if your presence in a negotiating session is at least 150% needed. Unless you—and only you—are needed to reach a negotiated outcome, do not even consider using the Vanish technique.

One way to use the Vanish technique is to be deliberately late. If there's a negotiating session scheduled, make sure everyone else has arrived, then show up for the meeting. This makes everyone wait for you. Next, leave quickly, before any agreement is reached. They cannot reach any solution without you. Since you're 150% needed, they must run after you to set up the next negotiating session. Since you are essential to the negotiation, they will

* run after you
* schedule the next negotiating session at a time convenient to you
* keep the negotiations as brief as possible so you will not vanish on them again

The Vanish technique is great if you're buying a car. Here's how it works. Once I really wanted to buy a particular automobile. I made the salesperson spend over three hours with me without ever agreeing on a price. Finally, I said, "Forget it," and started walking out the door of the showroom. The salesperson waited until I opened the door, and then he actually ran to ask me to come back in. I did, and we spent two more hours wrangling. I still did not budge a penny on the price I offered.

Finally, I told the salesperson he could keep the car, and I walked toward the door. The co-owner of the car dealership ran to block the door. He pleaded with me to stay. We spoke, and 10 minutes later I bought the car of my dreams—without spending one penny more than I first bid.

This Vanish technique produced a win-win outcome. The car dealership needed me 150%. Without me, it would not sell the car until another interested buyer walked in. Of course, the dealership had no idea when that might occur. In contrast, I represented a *real* prospect who had already—purposely—taken up hours of their time. As a result, the dealership had a huge need to sell the car to me.

The dealership won, since it made a sale. I won, because I purchased the car I desired at the exact price I felt willing to pay.

Backscratching—
The Oldest Technique in the Book

Backscratching—"You scratch my back and I'll scratch yours"—is probably the oldest negotiating technique on the face of the earth. It virtually assures win-win outcomes, mutual gain, and continued good relationships among those involved. The key reason backscratching is not used more is because many people feel that you should not ask for a favor in return for a favor.

In contrast, the high-achievers I studied were ready, willing, and able to ask someone to return a favor. These winners use such backscratching when they negotiate or need to influence someone.

The Backscratching technique is simple to use. You could say to the person you seek to persuade, "Remember the favor I did for you awhile back? I'd tremendously appreciate it if you would help me on this project."

THE DANGERS OF VERBAL AGREEMENTS

A final word on negotiating. Beware of verbal agreements. Samuel Goldwyn, the founder of Metro Goldwyn Mayer films studios, summed up the value of a verbal agreement when he declared, "A verbal contract is not worth the piece of paper it's printed on!" The movie tycoon's insightful remark points out a basic fact: Verbal agreements are often worthless.

For agreements where large amounts of money change hands, it is usually best to make a formal written agreement or contract. That minimizes future conflicts. It leaves few, if any, questions about exactly what the parties agreed in terms of

* goods or services to be provided
* fee for these goods or services

On the other hand, you would appear terribly bizarre if you convinced someone at your company to work on a project, and then said, "I want you to sign this agreement or contract to do that project."

However, if you need assurance that the person will not back out of the verbal agreement or will live up to the agreement, you still can do something. After agreeing with your co-worker about precisely what she will do, write a memo to that person detailing the agreement. In the memo spell out the who, what, when, and where to which that person agreed. Then, send the original memo to the person *and* "cc:" (courtesy copies) to the person's boss, colleagues, co-workers, or anyone else who may have an impact on her working on that project.

When the person receives your memo, a few things go on. First, she sees what she agreed to in writing. Second, if you misunderstood the agreement, she can call you (or write a memo of her own) to set the record straight. Third, by sending copies of the memo to others, there is pressure on her to carry out the agreement, since her boss, colleagues, or co-workers will notice whether she does what she agreed she'd do.

Tip: Here's some advice on how to get someone to sign an agreement. People feel more comfortable signing a paper you call an "agreement" than signing a paper you refer to as a "contract." A written "agreement" and "contract" are the same thing. However, a "contract" sounds more menacing than an "agreement" to many people. To them, an "agreement" sounds like, "Here's what we discussed and this form simply summarizes that discussion. So let's sign this agreement, since we already talked about it and verbally agreed to it."

So, always call it an "agreement" rather than a "contract." You'll find it much easier to get people to sign on the dotted line.

HOW TO CONCLUDE EVERY NEGOTIATION

To conclude this discussion, I will tell you what to do at the end of every negotiation. At the conclusion, always congratulate the other side for (1) getting the better end of the agreement *or* (2) doing a good job negotiating *or* (3) getting you to compromise more than you planned.

What do you gain when you congratulate the person? Since negotiating basically is carrying out part of a relationship, after you concluded negotiations, you'll probably need to deal with that person again. Therefore, you want him to leave feeling good about you so your next contact goes smoothly. Giving a small compliment helps the person feel that he made a wise choice. Remember, high-achievers compliment people much more often than underachievers. Doing so helps them get along with people and, importantly, negotiate, influence, and persuade with diplomatic agility.

CHECKLIST—
HOW TO NEGOTIATE, INFLUENCE, AND PERSUADE

Use the 2-step method of
_____ Step 1. Pace
_____ Step 2. Lead

Use negotiating techniques
_____ Ask for what you want
_____ Use simple pace-and-then-lead
_____ Use three types of questions
  _____ Open-ended
  _____ Yes-able
  _____ "Or"
_____ Overcome resistance and roadblocks
  _____ Step 1. Pace as soon as you hear resistance.
  _____ Step 2. Lead when the other person feels comfortable with you.
  _____ Step 3. As soon as you hear the other person resist again, immediately pace again.
_____ Other techniques are
  _____ Never ask "why?"
  _____ Robin Hood
  _____ Time is on your side
  _____ Brainstorm
  _____ Tom Sawyer
  _____ *Fait accompli*
  _____ Higher authority
  _____ Back burner
  _____ FBI

_____ Ultimatums

_____ Vanish

_____ Backscratching

_____ Use verbal agreements judiciously

_____ Conclude by complimenting the other side in the negotiation

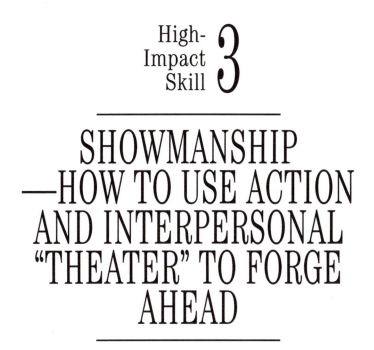

High-Impact Skill 3

SHOWMANSHIP —HOW TO USE ACTION AND INTERPERSONAL "THEATER" TO FORGE AHEAD

Showmanship makes quite an impression on both the executives and the managers who dole out career opportunities and the customers, clients, patients, and others who can decide where to take their business. High-achievers and underachievers differed dramatically in their abilities in this crucial area.

ATTITUDES ARE CONTAGIOUS—ACCENTUATE THE POSITIVE

The most glaring difference between high-achievers and underachievers is that high-achievers typically exude positive attitudes. Someone possessing a positive attitude overwhelmingly focuses on opportunities rather than drawbacks. Somebody with a positive attitude focuses on solutions rather than on problems.

Positive Attitudes Versus Negative Attitudes

Focus of *Positive Attitudes*	*Focus of* *Negative Attitudes*
Opportunities	Drawbacks
Solutions	Problems
"Can do"	"Cannot do"
Build bridges	Build roadblocks

Conversely, a person saddled with a negative attitude zooms in on possible drawbacks instead of opportunities. Also, those with negative attitudes tend to relish finding problems where others find solutions.

One eye-opening experience that helped me recognize these fundamental differences occurred when I looked at research on certain preemployment tests I developed. We had asked the same set of questions of high-achievers and underachievers doing the same jobs.

One question was: "Tell me about the worst experience you ever had in any job." Underachievers answered by telling us a variety of horrible experiences. Period. That is all.

The high-achievers also told us about utterly horrible experiences, but then the high-achievers would describe how they

* overcame the problem

* ended up better off for having gone through it

* avoided the problem in the future

All in all, high-achievers transformed their awful experiences into opportunities. They turned problems into something positive. Both groups lived through bad experiences. However, the high-achievers really got something out of them and developed into better people. In sharp contrast, the underachievers merely went through adverse experiences and gained nothing from them.

Remember the old computer phrase, "Garbage in, garbage out." That warns us that if we let our heads feed on negative garbage, we may find it hard to think and feel upbeat. If you feed yourself positive thoughts and feelings, and associate with cheerful people, you're much more likely to feel positive. With this in mind, here are some ways to do this.

First, avoid letting negative people or depressing news suck you into emotional or mental quicksand. I heard about a study in which scientists measured the biochemical energy in the brain used by people who are upbeat. The researchers also measured the biochemical brain energy expended by people who feel depressed. Interestingly, upbeat people used the same amount of biochemical brain energy as depressed people. Since you use the same amount of energy feeling positive or negative, it surely seems wiser to use your energy to pursue optimistic ends.

Second, attitudes certainly can prove contagious. You owe it to yourself and everyone you meet to make sure your attitudes seem worth catching.

I recently delivered a workshop at a company's management meeting. After my workshop, I enjoyed dinner with the company's president. This man radiated a delightful, upbeat, "can do" demeanor.

At one point during dinner, he asked me a profound question: "What do you think would happen to the vast majority of people if they listened only to positive, helpful news for just six months—and did *not* listen to any of the typical negative news?"

His question made me think. I bet people would feel better
* emotionally

❋ physically

People would achieve more and feel there were fewer limits on their potential to succeed. It would create a revolution in how people think and live.

Imagine, for example, somebody you know who acts awfully negative. This person cherishes opportunities to

❋ complain

❋ moan

❋ grumble about how horrible things seem

❋ point out problems to every solution you propose

This negative character is the type of person who improves the atmosphere in a room—when he leaves.

How do you feel when you spend time near this negative soul? Does hanging around this person leave you feeling excited, energized, motivated, and enthusiastic? Of course not—unless you are a glutton for punishment, a masochist, or both.

Negative people can drain us. When we allow ourselves to wallow in negative thoughts, we drain ourselves. That's why I strongly recommend that you

❋ surround yourself with positive people

❋ take positive actions

❋ read and watch positive, uplifting materials

Viewed from another angle, when you felt depressed, did you ever lift your mood by deliberately forcing yourself to think positive thoughts and feel positive emotions? Everyone has done that.

Let's reverse the situation. Have you ever felt on top of the world—when you spotted abundant opportunities and felt confident—and then purposely made yourself feel lousy? If you are a basically normal human being, you certainly wouldn't knowingly harm yourself.

Once, when I was in college, I babbled on and on for five minutes complaining about something to a friend. My friend finally could not take it any more, and said, "If some people did not complain, they would not exist."

That statement hit me between the eyes. It rang *so* true. I often remember that phrase when I feel like complaining or moaning about some difficulty I encounter. It helps remind me to search for opportunities rather than drawbacks, solutions rather than problems.

EXUDE CONFIDENCE

Half the trick of being successful is knowing what you're doing and doing it superbly. The other half of being successful is, when you don't know what to do, quickly figuring out what to do without ever letting on to anyone that you didn't know what to do in the first place.

The *swimming pool phenomenon* is the second showmanship tactic mastered by high-achievers. It works as follows: Someone asks a high-achiever to jump into a swimming pool and swim to the other side. She

* jumps into the pool
* somehow figures out how to swim to the other side
* actually swims to the other side

❋ gets out

❋ never fully reveals the extent to which she barely knew how to swim when she jumped into the pool

That describes the swimming pool phenomenon. It boils down to this crucial two-word phrase: *Exude confidence.* I found high-achievers consistently exude more confidence than underachievers.
I asked a famous lawyer what type of law he practiced. He replied,

I specialize in panic law. I always tell my clients that I know exactly what to do, even when I don't. After they leave my office, I *panic*, and then I stay up all night to develop a perfect and beautiful case for my client. It always works, but it wreaks havoc on my sleep patterns.

Think about this scenario. Imagine you are a manager, and you have two employees working for you. You can offer career opportunities to only one of your two employees.
First, imagine saying to your first subordinate, "I'd like you to carry out the such-and-such project" and that employee then responds by saying, "Gosh! Gee whiz, boss! I never did a project like that before, and I'm not too sure I can do that. It'll be hard for me to do it. Well, boss, um, well, um, I'll *try.*"
Then, imagine walking up to your second employee and making the same request. This employee replies, "Gosh! I never did a project like that before. But, don't worry. I'll figure out how to do it. If I have any questions I'll ask other people how to handle things. I'll look things up in magazines or books or manuals. I'll figure out how to do it. And don't worry, I'll have it on your desk by 5 P.M. on Friday."
Which employee would you consider more promising when career opportunities, such as a promotion or increased

responsibilities, opened up? Undoubtedly, the second employee—the one who exuded confidence.

What would you do if your first employee—the one who lacked confidence—was more intelligent than the more confident employee? You would probably still lean toward offering career opportunities to your second employee. That is the person who employed the "jump-into-the-middle-of-the-swimming-pool-and-then-figure-out-how-to-swim approach."

People using this approach get opportunities because people who exude confidence engender confidence in others. This includes the executives, managers, clients, and customers who can make or break careers. Such people go to the top of the list when career opportunities get doled out. So remember the swimming pool phenomenon and radiate confidence in everything you do.

Delete This Word from Your Vocabulary

Please recall a time you *tried* to do a project.

Actually, it is absolutely, totally, utterly, completely impossible to accomplish anything you only *try* to do. That is because you either do it or you do not do it. *Trying* to do anything does not *really* get anything done.

When you finish a project, did you *try* to do it? Or did you really do it? Obviously, you actually did it.

An amazing part of my research involved noticing how often high-achievers and underachievers used the word, "*Try*."

I discovered underachievers said the word "try" an average of eight times per day.

However, the high-achievers used the word "try" an average of only one time each day.

What an enormous difference!

Underachievers were vastly more likely to say things like "I'll *try* to finish that project this week" or "I'll *try* to do a good job." Saying "try" gave underachievers an escape hatch. If they accomplished their goals, that was fine. If they did not, they could fall back on the fact that they did not commit to doing anything. After all, they only vowed to "try."

In sharp contrast, high-achievers really do things and seldom leave themselves the escape hatch of only pledging to "try." Using the word "try" is like saying someone is "a little bit pregnant." Either you do it or you don't do it. Either you "try" *or* you really do it.

Based on this dramatic difference between winners and losers, I suggest you eliminate the word "try" from your vocabulary if you want to achieve a lot in your career and personal life.

JOIN THE TEAM

High-achievers *act* like team players. They *act* as if they enjoy group endeavors. In career terms, people who advance must use increasing amounts of teamwork as they progress. It goes with the territory. After all, moving ahead requires assuming more responsibility for *getting work done through people*. These people sometimes are subordinates whom the person controls by virtue of her management title. But, increasingly, higher-level professionals and managers must get things done through people over whom they exert no formal authority. Such participative endeavors require them to excel in at least three high-impact people skills, namely,

* Quickly making a good impression and developing rapport
* Persuading, influencing, and negotiating
* Teamwork

As for teamwork, my discussions with high-achievers revealed an interesting, seldom admitted fact. Specifically, some high-achievers who *act* as if they enjoy using teamwork told me they would rather not have to collaborate as much as they do. However, their ability to shine at teamwork played a key role in their ultimate success or failure. In other words, high-achievers need to *act* team-oriented to get ahead.

That explains why I refer to this showmanship technique as *acting* like a team player. It makes no difference how you feel about collaborating. All that counts in the final analysis is whether or not you really formed alliances with others to achieve goals that only teams or groups can accomplish.

ASSUME ULTRA-RESPONSIBILITY

I discovered that high-achievers overwhelmingly *take total responsibility* for both their successes and shortcomings. In contrast, I found that underachievers all too often perform the "victim" role with gusto. Underachievers were more likely than high-achievers to claim their predicaments were someone else's fault. For instance, they would declare someone

* gave them a hard time
* treated them unfairly
* "had it in" for them
* unjustly favored others

Many losers developed expertise at moaning about such real or imagined harm to their egos and careers. In fact, however, there are very few real victims, but some people are skilled at volunteering to play that role.

When they encounter difficulty, instead of taking responsibility for it and improving their situation, they complain that they're a victim. Someone gave them a hard time or they received unfair treatment. That may be true.

However, high-achievers—even when they get unfair treatment—still take responsibility and figure out some way to attain their goals. In contrast, underachievers are much more likely to sit back and say,

> Oh, woe is me. I'm a poor little victim. I can't control my life. I hope someone else will take care of poor little me.

The more you take responsibility for the dilemmas you face, the more likely it is that you can become a high-achiever. As the existential philosopher Jean-Paul Sartre stated, "Man is condemned to be free, because once thrown into the world he is responsible for everything he does." Winners in their careers and personal lives take being "thrown into the world" as an opportunity to take ultra-high levels of self-responsibility. Many people call that maturity or self-reliance.

Losers, on the other hand, waste tremendous amounts of energy and time searching for someone to take responsibility for their success, happiness, and destiny. Since that sounds like a childlike approach to life, many people refer to it as immaturity. High-achievers take the more strenuous, yet more rewarding, road by taking responsibility for all their accomplishments—and flops. They embody the motto, "If something could be, then it is totally up to me."

PUBLICIZE YOUR SUCCESSES

A showmanship method that divides high-achievers from underachievers is this: High-achievers publicize their successes to people who can make or break their careers. Yet underachievers who are equally intelligent and educated tend to show more humility. Such modesty may make them seem like nice, unassuming people, but it also keeps them out of the limelight. After all, it is hard to give career opportunities or business to people whose accomplishments no one knows.

I used a *get attention* technique myself to help land a bigger than normal bonus plus a promotion. My boss was not helping me get ahead. Yet I knew I was measurably improving my employer's bottom line. So I found out the company's chief financial officer (CFO), like the true Detail-Focused character he was, always strolled to the same coffee machine at *exactly* 10:30 each morning.

So, a few times a week I showed up at the coffee machine at 10:28—two minutes before he did. When he arrived at the machine, I told him details about the projects I directed that boosted the company's profits and produced great cost-benefit ratios. After impressing the CFO with my profit-improving talents, he arranged for me to receive a bonus quite a bit in excess of the bonus other high-achievers at my job level could earn.

Later, when the company reorganized, I got a promotion and a bigger job title. I probably would not have landed my sizable bonus and promotion if I had not *purposely* sought out and gotten the attention of an executive who could make or break my career.

Yes, it was calculating for me to do this. Yes, my strategy literally was planned down to the minute. Yes, I pinpointed exactly which executive could open doors for me. And, yes, it worked. My method won me the advancement and financial rewards I deserved.

This example does not in any way imply that you should brag. It does not suggest that you should do anything extreme. It merely stresses the fact that if decision makers do not know about the praiseworthy results you achieved, then do not expect them to find out through some magical means. Purposely let the people who can make or break your career know about your successes. And reap the benefits only they can offer you.

In fact, one reason some people do not achieve their potential is due to them incorrectly thinking certain school skills apply to the world of work. For instance, when you earned good grades in school, your teacher heaped attention on you. Such experiences led many people to think that they only needed to do well and they automatically would get attention and rewards. However, it definitely does not work that way when it comes to career success. Good work and valuable results are necessary, but not enough to get ahead. Instead, a person who produces results *and* gets attention from the right people earns recognition and the career rewards that go with it.

This prompts me to repeat the key principle embedded in this book:

> *Being competent in your work*
> *plus 75 cents*
> *will get you a cup of coffee.*
>
> *Being competent in your work plus making*
> *a fantastic impression on the people who count*
> *will get you at least $100,000 per year.*

Again, of course, $100,000 per year is a metaphor. High-achievers sometimes make more and sometimes less. However, the point remains. Human beings who tend to forge ahead invariably "advertise" their successes to get the attention they deserve and need to advance.

TOUCHY TOPICS—CAREER-LIMITING MOVES

High-achievers tend to avoid discussing volatile or divisive nonwork topics while they are at their jobs. Underachievers are more likely to venture onto such land mines. Topics to avoid include

* Politics
* Gender differences
* Race
* Their financial resources
* Bathroom humor
* Sex acts
* Religion
* Ancestry
* Nationality

Such touchy topics easily rub people the wrong way. As such, it seems best to avoid them, except when absolutely necessary.

This point strongly struck home when I worked for a company that hired a consultant to deliver a series of workshops. During the first workshop, the consultant commited a number of *faux pas*. He

* swore
* stereotyped the behavior of people of various ancestries
* compared a topic he presented to a sex act
* repeatedly referred to the women attending the workshop as "girls"
* frequently mentioned the large amount of money he charged for his consulting services

Amazingly, this consultant seemed totally surprised when he was told the organization canceled its agreement with him to conduct subsequent workshops. Perhaps he learned from the experience. Everyone attending his workshop certainly learned how *not* to act.

This consultant violated a vital showmanship principle:

Do not say or do anything
that may offend anybody.

Those who offend others, whether on purpose or not, pay dearly for it sooner or later. Generally, the payment comes out of a person's hide, career, bank account, or earnings potential.

You may well wonder what to do when others make a potentially offensive remark to you or in your presence. The answer: Ignore it, especially if the remark is typical of the way this person speaks or acts.

If the remark personally wounds you, or offends someone who does not readily speak up, you may want to comment in an unemotional tone, "It makes me uncomfortable when I hear sexist [foul, racist, ageist, nasty] remarks." By commenting in a matter-of-fact manner, you help the offending person avoid

* losing face
* getting too defensive

You also offer a lesson the person may not know.

Keep steady eye contact while making such a remark. This underscores your seriousness. In essence, be tactful. Do not degrade yourself by mirroring the offensive, unnecessary, unsophisticated, or closed-minded antics of others.

Once I attended a meeting at which someone, jokingly, cruelly stereotyped members of a specific group. The first two times he made these comments, no one, including me, said anything. However, I glanced around the room and noticed people looking uncomfortable and annoyed by his remarks.

When he made such a remark for the third time, I looked him in the eye and stated, in a steady and reserved voice, "It makes me uncomfortable when I hear remarks like that." You could hear the proverbial pin drop. No one said a word.

Finally, after a few moments of awkward silence, the offending person wisely chose to say to everyone, "I'm sorry. I didn't mean to offend anyone. I guess I shouldn't have talked like that. Now, let's get back to the meeting."

After the meeting, that person approached me. He thanked me for calmly pointing out what he had done. Also, he asked me to tell him if he ever again stepped over boundaries of tolerable behavior.

Perhaps he did not change the way he really thought about the group he ridiculed, but at least he now knows not to force others to listen to his biases.

Sometimes while delivering workshops, I mention these topics to avoid in the workplace. There is always one person who then asks me, "What else is there to talk about *if* I can't talk about politics, gender differences, ancestry, nationality, religion, money matters, sex, bathroom humor, and all those types of things?"

It always amazes me when people pose such questions. After all, millions of topics exist that do not throw gasoline on the fires of controversial or divisive subjects.

All in all, speaking tactfully is a valued art that affects careers. In fact, one company for which I conduct workshops coined an acronym for undiplomatic or crude speech. It's "*C-L-M*." That stands for *C*areer *L*imiting *M*ove. That's mighty true, isn't it? If someone's behavior turns off an executive or co-worker or customer, that person certainly committed a CLM.

NEVER RELIEVE YOUR OWN STRESS BY STRESSING OTHERS

The high-achievers I studied generally avoid relieving personal stress at somebody else's expense. In contrast, I found the underachievers more likely to spend some time easing their stress at the expense of someone else.

This could create a domino effect and foster a "Bite the Cat" game. It goes like this: A person humiliates his or her spouse who then hollers at the oldest offspring who slaps the youngest offspring who slaps the dog who then goes and bites the cat. People in organizations play this game with co-workers in a way that proves the meek most certainly will not inherit the earth. What screamers seek to pass off as decisiveness is really a grown-up version of a child's tantrum.

Similarly, high-achievers usually avoid arguing. One high-achiever I observed phrased it very well: "When you win an argument, you lose." Why? Because arguments practically beg for win-lose outcomes. Most arguments end with one person winning and the other losing, feeling humiliated, frustrated, degraded, and annoyed. When that happens, the person who lost often looks for a way to zap the person who won.

So it almost invariably proves wisest not to argue. Instead use the persuading, influencing, and negotiating techniques discussed earlier in this book to arrive diplomatically at win-win outcomes to conflicts.

Never relieve your stress at someone else's expense by

* yelling or screeching
* making humiliating comments
* mocking people's words or behaviors

Also, remember when you tell a joke in which you implicitly or explicitly put someone down, it is not very funny. People do laugh at such humor, but underneath their laughter they realize you could attack them, too, with humor. And no one *really* relishes that.

One truism I hear in many companies goes like this: "Be sure to be nice to people when you're on your way up." If you aren't, they could make

1. sure you get knocked off your high perch and tumble downward in your career
2. your life miserable as you descend in your career

For example, a company hired a woman as a secretary. As an exceptionally bright and ambitious person, she rose in the corporation to become the director of a key department. The company even paid for her to earn an MBA from a prestigious university's business school. She appeared every bit the superstar fast-tracker. Top management thought highly both of her and the staff she assembled and developed. Then, she announced she was leaving the company for a bigger job elsewhere.

She spent her last two weeks at the company in a nonstop tirade. Almost everybody she ever dealt with got told off. First, each of her staff members had their foibles, blunders, and everything else that caused her sleepless nights thrown in their faces. Then, she told her boss and other higher-ups how horribly they had treated her. Finally, she capped it off by scolding the janitor, complaining that her office never looked thoroughly clean. Everyone breathed a sigh of relief when she finally left. Years later, this person's ex-boss was asked to provide a reference for her. As you can imagine, it was hardly enthusiastic.

That highly skilled, motivated, capable person drowned her many years of superb work in a two-week temper tantrum. She felt better at the time; she released years of pent-up stress, but her behavior in her final days (daze?) of rage followed her for a long, long time.

We all want to rid ourselves of stressors. However, managing your stress at co-workers' expense can result in loss of a job, career opportunities, and your reputation. This is a high price to pay for momentary relief, and is sure to create new stressors after the old distressors vanish.

PAY 3 SINCERE COMPLIMENTS EACH DAY

This final showmanship tactic was discussed elsewhere. Specifically, high-achievers pay an average of *three sincere compliments each and every day*. In contrast, under-achievers typically pay no compliments. A major difference. Giving a compliment is easy to do. It takes mere seconds, and it even makes you feel good. Since "what goes around comes around," when you compliment someone, both career and personal goodies may come back in return.

CHECKLIST— SHOWMANSHIP—HOW TO USE ACTION AND INTERPERSONAL "THEATER" TO FORGE AHEAD

_____ Positive attitudes: Get them, nurture them, protect them, and exude them

_____ Remember "Garbage in, garbage out"

_____ Exude confidence

_____ Wipe the word "try" out of your vocabulary

_____ Teamwork pays

_____ Take ultra-responsibility for everything you do

_____ Purposely get attention from people who can offer you opportunities

_____ Avoid discussing divisive or volatile personal topics in the workplace

_____ Displaying poise under pressure gets you further than does letting off steam at the expense of other people

_____ Give 3 sincere compliments each day

High-
Impact **4**
Skill

HOW TO DELIVER PRESENTATIONS THAT IMPRESS

Once upon a time there was a department director who was very, very, very ambitious. He wanted to rise through the ranks to become an officer in his company. First, he would become a vice president. Then, he would advance to the position of a division president. And then...

So he excelled at managing. He *planned* well. He *organized* well. He *delegated* well. He *motivated* his staff well. He *controlled* his department's operations well.

Since he did everything so well, he smugly sat back and fully expected the company's officers, looking down from atop their corporate tower, to bestow a vice presidency upon him as a tribute to his great and bountiful wonderfulness.

Lo and behold, the corporate officers learned of this department director's overwhelming managerial magnificence and forthwith summoned him to their tower to deliver a presentation on his exceedingly glorious achievements.

The department director was thrilled. In his normal manner, he carefully planned his presentation down to its most Lilliputian detail.

The day of his presentation he arrived freshly scrubbed and wearing a perfect replica of the corporate officers' preferred uniform, that is, a clone outfit (see the section in Chapter 1, "How to Mirror Attire,") so he would visually fit in with his hosts.

Finally, his presentation time arrived. He stood up, walked to the front of the room, and gave it his best shot. Alas, his presentation could have been patented as the world's finest cure for insomnia. By his lackluster performance on stage, he lost any chance of becoming an officer in the company. Period.

This does not have to happen to you.

HOW DYNAMIC PRESENTATIONS
CAN OPEN DOORS FOR YOU

This actually happened. The bewildered department director later said, "I told them the facts. I just laid it all out for them, and told them. Plain and simple."

Indeed. And that was the problem. His presentation was too "plain and simple." That was his big mistake. No one wants to listen to anyone talk "plain and simple." The fact that an audience shows up means that the audience *expects* (1) useful information *and* (2) entertainment (although not necessarily in that order). Every audience expects the speaker to be well informed on his or her subject—otherwise, the person would not be speaking (usually true, but not always). But audiences also want and need to enjoy the presentation.

Think of two equally bright, informed, and insightful speakers you heard—one proved boring while the other came across as being enjoyable. Which one left you impressed and excited, as well as informed? More important, which speaker would you like to hear again? Which one would you recommend to others? Which one might you hire as a consultant or employee?

These questions beg the obvious. The speaker who arouses interest, enjoyment and enthusiasm—the one who knocks your socks off—comes out on top. This is true for people in all walks of life—consultants, corporate employees, and professionals of all types.

For instance, one large Southern city has two clinical (mental health) psychologists who wanted to develop huge private practices. Both chose delivering lectures before civic, PTA, and self-help groups as a great way to attract more patients. One of these clinical psychologists presents in a lively, bouncy, and informative manner. The other's presentations are only informative—plain and simple.

One of them now has a dozen other clinical psychologists and psychotherapists working full time for him. The other's appointment book is only one-half to three quarters full. He certainly does not attract anywhere near the number of patients needed to hire anyone to work for him, even on a part-time basis.

Compare what both did. *Same* marketing method: speeches before potential patients and referral sources. Same basic topics for their presentations. Both equally competent in their profession. Same city.

Yet, one drives a Jaguar; the other drives a midsized Chevrolet. One lives in the poshest part of this city; the other lives in a plain and simple middle-class neighborhood.

Only two words sum up the difference between the highly successful person and the less-than-successful person: *style* and *impact*.

According to a survey I conducted, audience members listening to a speaker talking on business or professional topics want the speaker to do the following, in this order:

Most wanted: Impress the audience
2nd most wanted: Entertain
3rd most wanted: Excite
4th most wanted: Inform
5th most wanted: Persuade

Isn't that amazing? Conveying information came in fourth out of five desired characteristics!! Theatrical or dramatic skills take precedence over getting information.

That's why this chapter will show you exactly how you can achieve high-impact skill number 4—delivering presentations that thoroughly impress whatever audience you address.

3 GUARANTEED WAYS TO FEEL CALM AND CONFIDENT

A nationwide survey uncovered the worst fears of people in the United States. Near the top of the list were such old standbys as fear of death and fear of disasters. Notably, the biggest fear of Americans was the fear of speaking in public. People are less scared of their own death than they are of delivering a presentation before a group of people! Telltale signs of "presentation phobia" include sweating, anxiety, dread, butterflies, and practically any other bothersome sensation imaginable.

Fortunately, however, everyone can feel calm and confident using these three easy-to-learn techniques:

1. Heavy Breathing

2. Proud Hands

3. Remembering one simple, yet profound, truth

"Heavy Breathing" to Relieve Pressure

The first technique's roots lay in a common meditation and relaxation technique. When you feel nervous, you invariably take shorter, shallower breaths. In contrast, when you feel calm, you take longer, deeper breaths.

To benefit from *Heavy Breathing*,

1. Take a *deep* breath.
2. Hold it for five seconds.
3. Slowly exhale.

Repeat this process a few times just before giving a presentation to feel calm. You can use the Heavy Breathing tactic without anyone ever noticing what you are doing.

Heavy breathing works by creating pressure and then releasing it. The *deep* inhaling pushes your lungs outward. This creates physical pressure on your chest muscles and chest wall. This pressure is the physical analogy of the "pressure" or stress some people feel before delivering a presentation. Exhaling relieves the physical pressure and, by extension, your emotional pressure.

Try it. You'll like it.

"Proud Hands" Technique to Create Buoyant Confidence

Another powerful way to feel calm and confident (sometimes even exhilarated) is the *Proud Hands* technique. It is based on the fact that a person's internal or mental images create that person's reality. Actresses, actors, sports superstars, and all sorts of professional people *imagine*—that is, picture in their minds—how they will act or succeed *before* actually going out and achieving their goals.

The same technique can make you feel buoyantly confident when giving a presentation. One way to do this is to use the Proud Hands technique. Here's how:

1. Close your eyes.

2. Imagine a time you felt extremely proud of yourself. Picture exactly how you looked. See in your mind how you stood, the expression on your face, and your posture.

3. In your mental picture, notice exactly how you hold your hands and arms while you feel extraordinarily proud of yourself.

4. With your eyes still closed, move your hands and arms into exactly the same position as they appear in your mental picture of a proud moment.

5. Keep your hands and arms in that position as you open your eyes.

6. Note exactly where your arms and hands are. That is your Proud Hands position.

Then, every time you want to inject confidence into your psyche during a presentation, start your speech with your arms and hands in your Proud Hands position. If you ever feel rattled during a presentation, immediately slip into your very own Proud Hands position. You will feel confident, because you have emotionally *programmed* yourself to feel proud when you use your Proud Hands.

And, as with Heavy Breathing, no one around you will notice anything strange. Reason: Proud Hands positions usually are fairly common ways of holding your hands and arms. So no one will have the slightest reason to know you are using a technique to help yourself feel more calm and confident.

For instance, in my Proud Hands position, I am holding my hands chest high, about shoulder width apart, with my palms facing toward each other. I inevitably begin each speech or workshop I deliver using this Proud Hands position. It helps me feel composed and assured in front of any audience.

One Simple, Yet Profound, Truth That Will Eliminate Nervousness

When I was about five years old, I was in a play. All the actors and actresses were about my age.

Before the play, I felt fine. However, almost all the other kids were crying and saying they were scared to go up on stage.

So I started crying to be like the other kids. Then, my mother told me a simple, yet profound, truth that instantly made me stop crying. In fact, her remark positively influences my public speaking performances to this day. She said, "There's absolutely nothing to worry about. The audience members do *not* know what you're supposed to say or do in the play. Even if you make a mistake no one will know it. So don't waste your energy and time acting nervous."

Interestingly, I played the role of a villain. My lines were supposed to be serious and not at all funny. However, when I delivered my lines, the audience broke into laughter. If that happened to another kid, he or she might have gotten scared or cried. But not me! I loved eliciting laughter so much so that I made up some lines on the spot and used them, even though I was not supposed to. The audience roared with more laughter. That upbeat audience response hooked me on

* using humor to get laughs
* not bothering to worry when I go "on stage" to deliver a speech or workshop

3 QUICK WAYS TO PREPARE GREAT PRESENTATIONS

By following these three steps, you can prepare first-rate presentations quickly.

1. "Reading" your audience to find out what presentation style will turn it on
2. Organizing your presentation using a fast and sure technique
3. Preparing visual aids to add luster and reinforce your message

"Read" Your Audience's Needs and Desires

A good presenter aims to please the audience. A mediocre presenter does not take the audience's possible reactions into account when preparing or delivering a presentation.

For example, a consultant was scheduled to address a business convention at 9 A.M. The consultant, of course, was an expert in her field and could talk about it with an air of authority. So the information she wanted to convey would be easy for her to present. But the audience would not be as easy to handle.

To make a long story short, the business group holding the convention (the specific type of business will go unmentioned for reasons that will be obvious) was chock-full of heavy drinkers. Since the consultant was scheduled to present at 9 A.M., she could not count on them to be alert. To get their attention, she began her speech by asking, "Has everyone had tomato juice and coffee yet? You'll feel better if you do. By the way, how do you feel this morning? How did you feel last night?"

The audience ate it up. They felt she was one of them. They never learned that the speaker was a confirmed teetotaler who never went to bars. She accurately "read" her audience and got them onto her side before she ever began her presentation.

Two main ways exist to "read" an audience to quickly figure out how to impress it. One way is the 4 Interpersonal Styles approach. The other is to know what people in different job levels tend to need and want.

As discussed earlier, most people use one of the following interpersonal styles:

* Results-focused
* Detail-focused
* Friendly-focused
* Partying-focused

A good presenter determines which focus or style his audience prefers. He then mirrors or copies the audience's preferred style. This is particularly important at the beginning of a presentation. It makes the audience feel the presenter is "with" them. After all, *human beings want to be around people who seem similar to themselves.*

The consultant addressing the business convention, as described earlier, did a stellar job of "reading" her audience. She figured out that at 9 A.M. at this convention, most of her audience would feel partying-focused. She fed right into it by talking in a partying-focused manner. She won their hearts, or at least their minds, by sounding so very like them. She focused on what her audience focused on.

It is good she did so, since that consultant is every bit a detail-focused type of person. If she had dived right into the details, as she wanted to, she would have seemed a galaxy away from her audience. Just because she knew the right answers did not mean her audience was prepared to ask the right questions or even listen. Because she "read" her audience, got onto their wavelength, she succeeded. In fact, she even picked up some lucrative consulting assignments based on the presentation she delivered.

The second useful way to "read" an audience takes into account the fact that typically, people at different job levels in an organization need different amounts of detail. In general, it works like this:

Major Concerns of Employees in Different Positions

Position of Employee	*Major Concern*
Executive	Whole picture
Middle manager	Large details
First-line supervisors and nonsupervisory employees	Small details

---

Specifically, executive-level employees tend to feel most concerned about the whole picture. They usually want to see the forest and not the individual trees, so to speak. Audiences of first-line supervisors and nonsupervisory workers focus on small details. After all, that is what the organization hires them to do. And middle managers land smack dab in the middle. They typically focus on large details, not quite the whole forest, but more than a tree.

For instance, executives frequently tend to concentrate on such things as broad business plans, industry trends, how the economy affects the executive's industry and company, and so on. If an executive focused on the itsy-bitsy, teeny-weeny details of how the company manufactures widgets or provides X service, then he or she literally would miss the whole picture while the company increases its likelihood of going down the tubes.

A nonsupervisory employee who works each day on the nitty-gritty of what the company produces needs to concentrate on how to produce whatever products or services he or she makes. If the employee spends too much time on whole picture issues, such as the company's long-range business plans, then the employee may overlook the tasks the employee needs to do.

Given this fact of business life, a presenter can tell a lot about how to present by determining the organizational level of the people who will compose the audience. For example, it is generally best to focus on the whole picture scenario when addressing a group of executives. In contrast, an audience of line employees may well prefer a more detail-oriented presentation. While exceptions exist for everything, these guidelines for accurately "reading" your audience work most of the time.

Organize Your Presentation in 30 Minutes or Less—Guaranteed

At this very moment, are you sitting down, so you won't fall over and hurt yourself? If so, read on.

Believe it or not, organizing a presentation is incredibly easy and generally should take less than 30 minutes. That even includes designing the transparencies or slides you will use.

Simply follow these steps:

Step 1. On one sheet of paper, print your presentation's TITLE.

Step 2. On another sheet, print the word "TOPICS" centered at the top of the sheet. Then, list the two to six main topics you will cover.

Step 3. For each topic, take a separate sheet of paper. (For instance, if you listed three main topics in step 2, then you need to take three sheets of paper.)

Step 4. At the top of each sheet (see step 3), list one of your main topics (from step 2), along with two to six of the points you will make about each topic.

Step 5. Take a new sheet of paper. Label it near the top with the word SUMMARY. On it, list the same two to six topics you listed on your TOPICS sheet in step 2.

Voilà!! You have just organized your presentation *and* designed your transparencies or slides. Now get your visual aids prepared to look sharp. You are almost ready to deliver your presentation.

The Easiest Way Ever Invented to Remember What to Say

From this moment on, you never again will fret about forgetting what you wanted to say. Absolutely, positively never!

How can I make such a statement with certainty? Very easily. Reason: Because you now possess, at your fingertips, the exact technique you need to help you remember what to say during any presentation.

And that is to *speak from transparency to transparency or slide to slide*. If you do this, you'll never again need to memorize a presentation or read a prepared text. Instead, you'll be able to use the phrases on each transparency or slide to *prompt* you or jog your memory on what to say next.

After all, each line on your visual aids is written to prompt you to remember an idea or fact you wish to convey to your audience. That is a major reason for using visual aids. So, how about using them to their fullest? To prompt you as well as reinforce your message to your audience, take advantage of your visual aids.

Create Visual Aids That Stand Out

Here's how to create effective visual aids, ones that will help jog your memory while you speak, as well as help your audience follow your presentation.

K.I.S.S. Your Audience

K.I.S.S. means *K*eep *I*t *S*hort and *S*weet. (Negative people and those with a hostile sense of humor define K.I.S.S. as *K*eep *I*t *S*imple, *S*tupid. They relish any chance they get to refer to others as dumb, unsuccessful, or "stupid.") To K.I.S.S., use the *Rule of Six*, that is,

✳ Write title and subtitles that contain no more than six words.

✳ Put six or fewer subtitles on each transparency or slide.

Doing this makes it easy for you to keep your visual aids uncluttered.

Put on a Show

When using transparencies, write on them during your presentation. Use felt-tipped pens specially made for writing on transparencies. You can buy such pens from office supply shops or art stores. The ink just wipes off with a slightly damp cloth or paper towel, so you can use the same transparency again and again. For instance, I deliver some of my speeches and workshops quite often. Some transparencies I write on during my presentations have been wiped clean well over a hundred times. Yet the words and graphics printed on the transparencies look as good as the day I made them.

If you use slides, use a flashlight to point at the slide. Keep one in your pocket; then, whip it out and surprise your audience with a flash of light as you point at select lines on your slides. After all, showmanship and surprises are essential parts of any presenter's bag of tricks.

Use Only Large Lettering

Transparencies and slides must contain *only large letters*. You have undoubtedly attended presentations at which the visual aids were difficult to read. In all likelihood, the print was too small. A small typeface is fine for letters, memos, and reports, but it is terrible for visual aids, since it makes your transparencies or slides unreadable. Keep in mind that just because you can read your transparency as you stand a few feet away from it, audience members 20 or more feet away from the screen may find it hard to read. The good news is that with the wide array of computer-generated graphics software available today, everyone can make effective visual aids, big enough for all audience members to read.

Audio-Visual Aids Add Interest

When properly used, audio-visual aids add interest, appeal, and poignancy to a presentation. They illustrate points and provide lifelike examples for the audience. The two main types of audio-visual aids are videotapes and audiotapes.

Videotapes typically elicit better responses than do audio recordings. The reason is simple. Videos hit two senses, vision and hearing, while audio recordings strike only one sense, hearing.

It's important to know how to use videos to get the impact you want. They are meant to be part of a presentation, not the entire presentation. As good as they may look, your audience came to experience a warm body talking to them, not a spool of plastic threading through a video player.

Keep some or all lights on while playing videos, so no one falls asleep. Speaking of sleep, after lunch, most people feel drowsy. So presenting right after lunch opens the speaker up to an audience with food-induced lethargy. Showing a brief, lively video often gives the crowd time to digest lunch. It also assures you of a more awake and alive audience.

In addition to using videos to illustrate serious points in a presentation, you can also rent or buy many humorous videos. These add vibrancy and bounce to any presentation. For example, I sometimes use a particular video during talks to salespeople. This video shows a famous cartoon character delivering a hyperemotional presentation on how selling is as American as apple pie. He builds himself into such a frenzy that he concludes by ripping off his suitcoat, tie, and shirt while wildly screaming, "SELL!!!!!" over and over again. This amusing video loosens up the audience and sets a fun tone for the more down-to-earth parts of my presentations on how to sell more or deliver persuasive presentations.

Another video I use presents a "Twilight Zone"–type version of listening skills. It starts with a number of outrageous, funny vignettes about bizarre situations poor listeners could get themselves into. It then ventures into a series of clear, easy-to-apply scenes illustrating how to use specific crucial listening skills. The video provides a tremendous mix of colorful humor with highly pragmatic examples. It works wonders during my presentations on communications skills, negotiating, and sales techniques.

A third humorous video I use helps me summarize my interviewing skills workshop. This seminar teaches managers how to interview and evaluate job candidates. At the end of the seminar, I could give a serious synopsis of the various interviewing and applicant assessment skills participants learned.

Instead, I show a comical video on how *not* to interview a candidate. This video shows an interviewer doing each step of the interview wrong and exactly the opposite of what I just taught in the workshop. Audience members find it entertaining and funny. Also, they instantly recognize how the bad interviewing skills shown in the video sharply contrast with the proper interview skills I taught them in the workshop.

THE 3 DOs OF FIRST-RATE PRESENTATIONS

DO—Move Your Body

Showmanship is essential to a presentation. Most speakers stay glued behind a podium. I call that "podium barricade." Not only do they hide back there, but their lack of movement eliminates an important physical outlet for their energy.

Good presenters move while presenting. They walk into the middle of the audience. They move toward questioners and then away from them. Such movement serves several important purposes.

A speaker's physical actions convey vibrancy to their audiences. Active presenters look alive and lively. They even *feel* alive to the audience. Anyone brave enough to move while presenting tends to appear confident to everyone watching. After all, such a speaker certainly does not hide behind a podium like a scared rabbit.

It also helps to move your arms and hands while presenting. Few sights are stranger than an adult speaking before an audience with his arms and hands plastered to his sides. You should use your hands and arms to motion, point to visual aids, or make a point. In other words, use energy in a poised, dramatic way.

For instance, when you say something is "big," make sure you hold up your hands and make a motion to convey nonverbally something that is big. Or, if you say something is "small," then hold up one hand and use your thumb and index finger to convey something small.

From experience, I have also found that audience size must be taken into account when making hand and arm motions. For instance, I generally deliver my seminar on conducting productive meetings to groups of 40 or fewer participants. At one point in the workshop, I make a point accompanied by a particular arm motion that always simultaneously conveys a key point and gets a laugh from the audience. Once, however, when I delivered this workshop to

150 people, that comment and motion did not get a laugh from anyone sitting more than 30 feet away from me. It suddenly dawned on me that my bigger-than-usual audience required bigger-than-usual gestures for me to drive points home and get everyone to see my movements. From then on, I purposely made my gestures much, much bigger than I normally do. Then, everyone in the workshop was able to see my motions, and they added to the seminar's effectiveness.

DO—Use Your Voice for Maximum Impact

Here is a surefire technique to make yourself sound more stimulating: *Speak 50–100% louder than you normally do.*

When you speak more loudly than usual, a few useful things happen. First, you automatically sound more enthusiastic. Second, your audience pays more attention. Third, you feel less tense, since your louder voice lets out energy you might otherwise may keep trapped inside yourself.

You also can raise and lower your vocal volume to create an intriguing effect. You could speak loudly and then practically whisper. Show emotion. If you want a point to hit home, then *sound* like it is important. Sound like you feel emotionally and intellectually committed to the point.

To get ideas on how to use your voice for maximum impact on your audience, ask yourself this question: If audience members could not see my visual aids and my movements, what could I do with my voice to rivet their attention and enthusiasm onto me? Then, do just that with gusto.

DO—Copy Professional Speakers

Combine Physical and Vocal Movements

Tremendous presenters combine voice and body movements to make intriguing, even startling, positive effects on their audiences.

One best-selling author and management guru uses them very well. He begins his presentations, complete with gorgeous slides, at the podium, but then he quickly wanders while talking into the middle of his audience. He roars main points at earshattering volume. Then, two seconds later he practically whispers into the microphone his follow-up comment. The man pierces the air with his index finger to dynamite emphasis into his main points. Every once in awhile, he puts his hand on an audience member's shoulder, looks at him or her, and then directs 30 seconds or so of his presentation to this one audience member. This author-consultant is a sought-after orator. Once, when someone asked how he plans a speech, he simply replied,

Show business. It's all show business. I know my topic. My audience knows I know my topic. So all that's left for me to do is act, to be theatrical. I have a really good time doing it, and so does my audience.

HOW TO TACKLE DIFFICULT QUESTIONS, COMMENTS, AND HARD-TO-PLEASE AUDIENCE MEMBERS

Presenters seldom speak and then rush off the stage or out of the room. They usually answer questions and get comments tossed at them. Perhaps hardest to handle is an audience member who just wants to give you a hard time. While the questions, comments, and difficult people may be bothersome to everyone in the audience, the presenter will still be judged on how tactfully and smoothly he or she handles these situations.

For instance, if a speaker gives a great talk and then acts nasty toward an obnoxious audience member, people may leave with the speaker's lack of diplomacy and immaturity indelibly imprinted in their memories.

The image of two gladiators verbally hacking away at each other is the impression the audience would keep. The great presentation may well take a distant second place in their memories. Given these likely dilemmas, here are pointers on how you smoothly can handle questions, comments, and hard-to-please people.

How to Adeptly Handle Difficult Questions

This can be simple. First, listen carefully to the question. Second, repeat or paraphrase the question *only if the audience did not hear it*. Move or look away from the questioner so that person does not become the focus of attention. Then, as the presenter, you can (1) answer the question, (2) throw the question back to the questioner to answer, or (3) ask the audience for answers to the question.

If the questioner persists in talking or asking questions, then you may diplomatically and calmly say, "Let's give others a chance to ask questions now" or "For me to finish the presentation in the allotted time, I need to continue with the presentation. I hope we'll have time for more questions later." Keep it as simple as that.

How to Smoothly Handle Negative Comments

The mere fact someone displays the guts to get up in front of a bunch of people to give a talk invites comments. The situation seems so extremely juicy that it inevitably begs for an audience member to make comments—both pro and con. Hearing favorable comments lifts up the speaker with a smug sense of satisfaction, an "I've got them wrapped around my finger" confidence.

But sometimes an audience member seeks to destroy the speaker's entire premise with arguments, disagreements, pickiness, and pettiness. When that happens, the speaker can become open game for others in the audience. In fact, one well-known person in the job-hunting skills field recommends job hunters attend speeches. At the speech's conclusion, this expert recommends the job hunter stand up and say something to burst the speaker's balloon. Why do that? Because then the job hunter becomes the center of attention in the room. After the speech, other audience members will want to talk with him or her, and that spells potential contacts for jobs.

I once attended a speech skillfully delivered by a famous political commentator. She pulled together many observations and made some fascinating hypotheses about international political events. When the speech ended, the presenter asked for questions. A person in the front row put up his hand, and the speaker called on him. The questioner rose, looked the presenter straight in the eye, and emphatically stated, "So what!"

The speaker looked stunned. She asked the questioner, "So what, what?"

The questioner glared at her, and replied, "You made a lot of conjectures, you gave a lot of facts, but so what? What difference could your ideas possibly ever have on the *real* world?"

The questioner succeeded at figuratively sticking a knife into the presenter's heart and then slowly turning the knife as the presenter dangled in the wind.

Lo and behold, the questioner was the well-known job-hunting expert. Indeed, after the question-and-answer period, more people wanted to talk to him than to the presenter. His suggested tactic worked just as he predicted.

Luckily, presenters need not fear. Methods exist to handle almost every comment. The speaker simply can agree and continue, or paraphrase and continue. It is possible to encourage audience discussion by asking something like, "What are the thoughts of other people here?"

However, the most skillful reaction is to make an artfully vague response and then continue. As you may recall, an artfully vague response is a verbal sleight of hand in which the speaker's comment or reply leaves the other person feeling he or she was correct, understood, or agreed with. However, a closer look at the response reveals that the statement was neutral at best about the other person's comment. Examples of artfully vague responses to a comment by an audience member are "That's a point" or "You have an idea there!"

Upon hearing such a response, the person who made the comment tends to feel understood or justified in his or her comment. Actually, the responder certainly did not necessarily understand nor agree. After all, *any* comment makes "a point" or conveys "an idea." The presenter did not bother to say it was a ridiculous point or lousy idea. He or she just acknowledged that the questioner had made "a point" or expressed "an idea." Also, by using such artfully vague responses, the presenter retains control of the audience and may garner respect from the person who made the comment.

Secrets of Diplomatically Handling Hard-to-Please Audience Members

The most difficult audience members sometimes look the most respectable. For example, a company president served as master of ceremonies (MC) at a huge luncheon at a major city's chamber of commerce. The luncheon speaker was the managing partner of a highly respected consulting firm. His topic was "How to Use a Consulting Firm Wisely."

When the consultant finished the speech, audience members asked quite a few questions. Then, the MC stood up and asked, "I *insist* that you tell all of us here today how we could spend much less money using *your* consulting firm?" The nasty tone of the question sent a chill and a queasy hush over the audience. The MC was not trying to be funny; the speaker and the audience members knew it all too well. To make matters worse, in front of the over 200 audience members, the MC proceeded to grill the speaker nonstop for 10 minutes.

Not every difficult person needs to hone his or her craft in front of large audiences. An offensive audience member could be a competitor or rival who wants to prove he is better than you. It could be someone who simply lacks a sense of manners and propriety. Or it could be an uncouth person who heartily disagrees and just does not know how to conduct a civilized discussion.

Regardless of the culprit's reasons or goals, any speaker can handle such hard-to-please people with tact and diplomacy. To begin, the presenter must *always* appear to be in command, poised, and unruffled. To do so,

* Act totally unshaken.

* Do not flinch.

* Act "understanding."

* Stand up, if you are sitting down, to emanate an air of authority.

Then, after displaying the epitome of poise, grace, and control, do exactly what you would otherwise do to handle negative comments—(1) express agreement, (2) paraphrase, or (3) give an artfully vague response—and then continue.

Or you could encourage audience discussion with an open-ended question such as, "What do others in the audience think?" Warning: You should encourage audience discussion only if it seems as if the audience is on your side. Otherwise, it could produce results that you'd do well to avoid.

HOW TO ENCOURAGE AND CONTROL AUDIENCE PARTICIPATION

A presenter plays a dual role. First and foremost, the presenter serves as the center of attention. Almost as importantly, the presenter must assume implicit master of ceremonies duties. MC responsibilities encompass both encouraging audience participation so everyone feels part of the event and controlling the length and depth of audience participation. Such MC duties become obvious during practically every presentation. Audiences—whether of 5 or 500 people—contain members who want to ask a question, make a comment, or say something.

The savvy presenter should not try to avoid such people. However, the smart presenter must keep in mind at all times that it is the presenter, and no one else, who must take control and keep control of the timing and tone of the presentation. As soon as someone else in the room assumes a controlling posture, the presenter becomes a pawn in that other person's game plan. So the winning presenter must know how to take control of the audience and exercise control in a subtle, sophisticated, and poised manner in order to make a successful presentation.

Encouraging audience participation proves fairly easy with any but the most lethargic and shy groups. The most direct method is for the presenter to begin his or her presentation with a brief announcement that questions or discussion will be solicited at a certain point in the speech. Then, the presenter can request discussion when he or she wants it, and usually will get it since the audience knows it is expected. Once discussion begins, the presenter can just let people talk. That sets a ground rule in the audience's mind that it is all right to talk. Even then, however, the presenter must *control audience participation.* Two physical tactics and two verbal strategies will help you to perform this feat quite effectively.

As for the physical techniques, the presenter can control audience participation by taking either of the following actions when an audience member speaks up:

1. Standing up—this demonstrates an unspoken, but greater, sense of authority than sitting during questioning or discussions

2. Flipping the overhead transparency projector (or slide projector) off when an audience member starts speaking and, later, flipping the projector light on to show another visual aid when the presenter wants the person to wind down. The light serves as a cue to start or stop talking.

The easiest verbal technique involves setting time limits. An amazingly easy and successful way to get audience members to stop talking is to say something like,"We have only 10 minutes left for my presentation, and I'm going to need practically every minute of it to finish on time. So let's continue." The presenter then proceeds with the prepared talk.

WHAT *NOT* TO SAY

A very-high-level executive delivered a speech to a large group of employees whom he referred to as his "troops." He apparently was in a World War II mood that day, since he began by telling them a "joke" about a Kamikaze pilot, complete with a mock Japanese accent. Only a few people in the audience laughed, or perhaps they just sighed at his poor taste.

To rebound, he told the group it "*must* laugh at my jokes!" and then clicked his heels together and gave a "Heil, Hitler" salute, as if to emphasize his demand. A deathly silence followed this display of poor taste. Flustered, the corporate officer realized his "humor" wasn't working and retreated into his prepared remarks. You can imagine his employees' reactions!

The moral of this real-life example is

> *Do not say or do anything that*
> *you would not want to see*
> *printed on the front page of a newspaper.*

If something you say fails that acid test, then you may well regret it later. Such errors are hard to live down. They tend to leave bad feelings that could come back to haunt a presenter.

To avoid such pitfalls, here is a list of topics you would do well *not* to mention in your presentations:

* Sex
* Gender differences
* Politics
* Unrelated philosophical issues
* Nationality
* Ancestry
* Income
* Slander or gossip
* Religion

Mentioning these items often evokes laughter which lulls the presenter into a false sense of comfort. However, such comments invariably bother some people in an audience, and it is always better for a presenter to build bridges with an audience than to fire buckshot into their faces. Presenters must always keep in mind that

A major goal of any presentation is to make a fantastic impression.

Of course, you know offended audience members will not be favorably impressed.

HOW TO SUCCEED AT GIVING THE 2 MAIN TYPES OF PRESENTATIONS

Presenters deliver two main types of presentations: (1) informative presentations and (2) persuasive presentations. The steps needed to plan, prepare, and deliver each type of presentation are laid out here. All the pointers discussed so far provide the foundations upon which these two types of presentations are created and delivered.

Informative Presentations

An informative presentation, as the term implies, conveys information. Preferably, of course, the speaker transmits the material in an exciting, impressive, and somewhat entertaining manner.

Here are the six main steps:

Step 1. *"Read" Your Audience.* Determine its chief style from among the 4 Interpersonal Styles or its status level, and thus your audience's corresponding focus.

Step 2. *Organize Your Presentation.* This should take you less than 30 minutes using the procedure explained earlier in this chapter.

Step 3. *Create Visual Aids.* Transparencies, slides, and handouts are appropriate.

Step 4. *Practice.* Say it aloud or, if you feel embarrassed talking to yourself,[1] run through the visual aids while silently practicing what you will say. Even many seemingly off-the-cuff speeches are practiced.

Step 5. *Feel Calm and Confident.* To help feel confident, use the Heavy Breathing or Proud Hands techniques, and remember that the audience does not know if you make a mistake.

Step 6. *Do It!* Just get up there, and deliver your presentation. Speaking becomes easier and more exciting the more you do it. So dive in head first. *Warning:* Giving presentations can become habit forming.

Persuasive Presentations

Persuasive presentations take more planning, plotting, poise, and diplomacy. A speaker needs to be agile to influence a group that may or may not wish to be convinced of anything. Just as the risk is higher, so are the potential rewards, both materially and emotionally.

The following steps tend to work best:

Step 1. *"Read" Your Audience.*

Step 2. *Organize Your Presentation.* Since you need to persuade your audience, you must

❋ Include your opponents' ideas. Show that you understand the rationale behind their ideas.

---

[1]Once, when I walked into a room and heard a woman talking to herself, I said to her, "Oh, you're talking to yourself." She looked up at me and replied, "Of course I am. I know a good conversationalist when I hear one."

✳ Give strong reasons why your opponents' ideas are good. At first glance, this may seem akin to suicide, but actually it helps build rapport, trust, and comfort.

✳ Compare and contrast your opponents' ideas with your ideas.

✳ Focus on similarities that bridge the two viewpoints, or focus on small differences.

✳ Present a heavy dose of the benefits to be gained by the audience from your ideas.

Step 3. *Talk with Your Opponents. Before* your presentation, speak to people who oppose your ideas. See if you can reach understanding, compromise, and agreements. This is easier before a presentation than during it.

Step 4. *Practice Your Presentation.* Make sure you play devil's advocate, too, to find out how well your perspective stands up under attack.

Step 5. *Feel Calm and Confident.* Use the techniques described earlier.

Step 6. *Arrive Early.* Greet audience members as they arrive. Chat with them in a friendly—preferably chummy—way. This helps recruit allies—people who are, at least, favorably disposed to you if not to your ideas.

Step 7. *Do It!* Persuasive presentations are never dull. In fact, they can be quite hair-raising at times. With practice, they can also be exceedingly exhilarating.

CHECKLIST—
HOW TO DELIVER PRESENTATIONS THAT IMPRESS

_____ Give your audience what it really wants

_____ Impress audience

_____ Entertain

_____ Excite

_____ Inform

_____ Persuade

_____ Feel calm and confident

_____ Heavy Breathing

_____ Proud Hands

_____ Remember—the audience probably won't even know if you make a mistake

_____ Prepare your presentation

_____ "Read" your audience's needs and desires

_____ Organize your presentation in 30 minutes or less

_____ Prepare visual aids

_____ Practice speaking from transparency to transparency (or slide to slide)

_____ Employ visual aids

_____ K.I.S.S.

_____ Rule of 6

_____ Put on a show

_____ Large letters

_____ Videos

_____ Avoid "podium barricade"

_____ Move your body while presenting

_____ Speak 50–100% louder than you normally do

_____ Be theatrical

_____ Handle questions, comments, and hard-to-please people with tact and confidence

_____ Encourage and control audience participation

_____ Never say or do anything that you would not want to see printed on the front page of your hometown newspaper

_____ Appropriately deliver

  _____ Informative presentations

  _____ Persuasive presentations

HOW TO CONDUCT HIGHLY PRODUCTIVE MEETINGS

According to my research, the ability to conduct highly productive meetings is among the top six high-impact skills consistently displayed by high-achievers. It is the fifth most important communications skill.

To illustrate how important this is, think back to a *highly productive* meeting you attended. What impression did you develop of the meeting's leader? Did you consider the leader a pushover or fool? Probably not. Did the meeting leader come across as a well-meaning soul who seemed unable to lead or organize? Or did you view the leader as a person in control, organized, and conscientious about accomplishing the meeting's objectives? If this was your view, you undoubtedly considered the meeting's leader a winner in a number of ways.

Now, look at the other extreme: Imagine a highly *un*productive meeting. How did you feel by the end of *that* meeting? Excited, enthusiastic, on top of the world, and knowing exactly what to do? Probably not.

It's easy to predict how you felt. The *un*productive meeting left you bursting at the seams vowing to avoid such blundering wastes of time, energy, effort, and—yes!—money.

Now, think about the impression you formed of the leader of that unproductive meeting. Did that person seem poised, confident, in control, and organized? Probably not. In all likelihood you felt that person's leadership abilities had vanished into thin air (if they ever existed) and that organization was a never-heard-of concept.

In a nutshell, a professional or businessperson who leads an unproductive meeting appears inept to the attendees. That sort of meeting leader may never get mistaken for a winner. After all, would you entrust your time, energy, and effort to that sort of person at another meeting?

There, in brief, is a message about why it is so very important to conduct meetings in such a way that all participants leave knowing deep in their hearts that the meeting proved highly productive. People with such superb meeting leading skills are *Ringmasters* in the grandest sense. A circus ringmaster keeps all the acts flowing smoothly in an organized and synchronized way. The circus ringmaster simultaneously keeps the audience entertained, enjoying themselves, and in awe of how effortlessly the entire show unfolds.

Similarly, an adept meeting leader (Ringmaster) in business and the professions also orchestrates the meeting in a smooth, effortless way to fulfill the needs, interests, and enjoyment of all participants.

Before you can be a successful Ringmaster, you must first understand what a meeting is and why meetings are held. Then you'll be able to understand precisely what a Ringmaster does to direct a highly productive meeting.

WHAT IS A MEETING?

Many people think a meeting is a mighty big to-do. They picture many people in a large room. In contrast, other people view a meeting as something as minor as bumping into someone in a corridor. For the purpose of succeeding in your career, we define a meeting as *any time two or more people discuss topics that result in planning or carrying out productive actions.* People hold meetings to accomplish goals. Therefore, a meeting could be anything from a one-to-one discussion in a person's office to a get-together of many people. This chapter focuses mainly on the skills needed to lead meetings of groups of people. However, essentially the same techniques apply to a meeting of only two people.

Improving Your Organization's Bottom Line— The Main Reason for Most Meetings

Money and meetings go hand in hand. What I mean by that is best illustrated by example: Businesses hold meetings to figure out how to make more money or, conversely, to uncover how to spend less money. Therefore, marketing people may meet to decipher marketing, positioning, demographic, industry, regulatory, or technological trends to decide how best to create a market niche or grab a bigger market share. Manufacturing people get together to figure out how to produce more widgets for less money. And so on.

At this point, people who work in "not-for-profit" or "nonprofit"[1] organizations may protest, "Well, meetings could mean money in for-profit organizations. However, in my not-for-profit organization, meetings fill a 'higher good' and are not simply focused on making money."

An art historian from an art museum expanded on this point at one of my seminars. I asked her to describe a meeting she recently attended at the museum. She said she and other museum officials and experts met to decide what works of art the museum should acquire. "You see," she

---

[1]Actually, there is no such thing as a nonprofit organization, since *any* organization that does not make a profit in some way would go out of business from lack of money.

pointed out, "acquiring art promotes a 'higher good'. It's not just about making more money."

I agreed that museum art collecting definitely fulfilled a `higher good.' "But," I continued, "give me three good reasons why your museum should acquire more art. It already has a glorious collection."

"That's simple," she replied. "To develop an even finer, more well-rounded collection and to attract more visitors to the museum. Also, finer art collections attract more well-heeled benefactors for the museum."

I pointed out that "attracting more visitors" is a euphemism for "getting more *paying* customers" to tour the museum. As for lining up more "well-heeled benefactors," that merely meant getting more people to donate more funds to the museum. I rested my case.

A physician who attended one of my *Productive Meetings Workshops* mentioned that he holds case conferences to discuss cases to (1) impove his staff's treatment skills, and (2) continue his clinic's stellar reputation so even more patients come to it for diagnosis and treatment. Again, even meetings for a `higher good' in healthcare tend to boil down to figuring out how to make more money.

Given the meeting-money connection, it is crucial for astute business and professional people to understand and use a type of *cost-benefit analysis* when holding meetings. A meeting typically proves valuable when the benefits produced from the meeting outweigh the meeting's cost.

Typical meeting *costs* include the following:

1. Salaries and benefits paid to meeting participants during the time they attend a meeting

2. Meeting facility use, such as rent, lighting, and heat

3. Money that participants do not earn or productivity lost while attending a meeting

In contrast, potential meeting *benefits* include

1. Increased productivity and efficiency, that is, making more services or products for less money
2. Lowered costs
3. More sales

For example, let us calculate costs and benefits for a two-hour meeting of ten employees. In this example,

1. Participants each earn $25 an hour in salary and benefits
2. It costs $10 to pay for the use of the meeting room
3. Each employee normally brings in an average of 200% of his or her salary and benefits for a total of $50/hour[2]

Given these expenses, the cost of holding the meeting is as follows:

1. Salary and fringe benefits =
   10 employees × 2 hours × $25/hour/employee = $500
2. Facility use = $10
3. Money not made during meeting =
   10 employees × 2 hours × $50/hour = $1,000

Total meeting cost = $500 + $10 + $1,000 = $1,510

Total meeting benefits = ?

Therefore, for this $1,510 meeting to prove beneficial, it better result in at least $1,511 or more (preferably lots more) of one or more of these financial factors:

* Increased productivity and efficiency
* Lowered costs

---

[2]For instance, a general guideline in many consulting firms is that a professional on staff, or consultant, must bring in 150% of his or her salary and benefits cost just for the consulting firm to break even on that person.

✴ More sales

Lawyers and taxi drivers sum it up this way: "*The meter always is ticking.*" The taxi driver turns on his meter, running up a rider's tab all the time. So time literally equals money for the cab driver.

Similarly, many lawyers and other experts who sell their brains charge clients by 1-minute (1/60-hour), 6-minute (1/10-hour), 10-minute (1/6-hour), or 15-minute (1/4-hour) increments. For example, if a professional charges clients for 15-minute increments, a client who converses for 14 minutes gets charged the professional's 1/4-hour fee for using up to 1/4-hour of time. A client who uses 16 minutes is charged for 1/2-hour for using up two 1/4-hour time slots, or fraction thereof.

Regardless of how you charge for your time, goods, or services, time equals money for the wise person. Extraordinarily successful people reap the largest harvest from this unblushingly capitalistic phenomenon.

CHARACTERISTICS OF A HIGHLY PRODUCTIVE MEETING

It certainly looks, sounds, and feels important to conduct a superproductive meeting. But what exactly does a leader need to do to produce such a superbly crafted event? The answer is twofold, with the first answer very general and brief, while the second answer is more specific and longer.

In general, a successful Ringmaster performs these three main feats:

1. Starts *every* meeting *on time* and ends *on time*.

2. Orchestrates the meeting. The Ringmaster simultaneously shows *organization* and *control over* the entire event.

3. Always makes sure the meeting's *goals and agenda* are accomplished.

It really is that simple. There is no magic to a good meeting. Instead, the event depends on a conductor who confidently melds together people with diverse psyches, motivations, and aptitudes into a smooth-playing orchestra.

The next step is to dive into specific steps and skills needed to conduct highly successful meetings.

5 STEPS TO A SUCCESSFUL MEETING

A successful meeting results from carrying out these five main steps:

1. Planning the meeting
2. Organizing the agenda
3. Conducting the meeting
4. Concluding the meeting
5. Following up after the meeting

Step 1: Plan the Meeting

Beware and Be Aware:
Your meeting begins even before it begins

Before the meeting occurs, its leader must plan it. That means the leader must

* Determine the meeting's goals or purpose; and
* If it is a "formal" meeting, send an announcement memo to each participant

Create Meeting Goals

Here, the meeting leader must clearly and succinctly decide precisely what must be accomplished by the meeting.

That is, what are the meeting's objectives or desired end results? For example, a meeting's goal could center on sharing information or planning a project.

Send an Announcement Memo

This is the leader's first opportunity to organize and structure the meeting. If possible, only invite people who can help accomplish the meeting's goals. You can send a "cc:" (courtesy copy) of the announcement memo to select people you do not invite but who may want to know about the meeting. Or you can ask them if they want to attend.

After deciding on the meeting's players, write the memo. Keep the memo brief but do include

1. List of participants

2. Meeting goals or purpose

3. Starting and ending times

4. Preparation required, if any

5. Agenda (optional)

A sample meeting announcement memo appears in Exhibit 1.

Exhhibit 1

To: John Deere
        Mary Moose
        Ford Mustang
        Bif Liver

From: Jon Doe

Subject: Meeting

As discussed with each of you, we will meet to plan how to establish a new Science Museum exhibit on local wildlife species. Our meeting takes place on Tuesday, June 11, 10–11 A.M. at Grange Hall in Meeting Room Z.

Please bring your address books so we can start a campaign to enlist your friends and colleagues to our cause.

Here is our meeting's agenda:

1. Purpose of Meeting
2. Listing Local Wildlife Species
3. Planning Fund-Raising Drive
4. Starting a Campaign to Enlist New Members
5. Wrap-up

See you there!

Step 2: Organize the Agenda

After calling the meeting, the leader must draw up its agenda. As previously stated, for the leader *the meeting begins even before the meeting begins*. With the meeting goals clearly in mind, the agenda is a cinch to create. Simply list the (1) topics to be discussed and (2) time limits. For example, Exhibit 1 shows the meeting announcement memo for a meeting to set-up a wildlife exhibit at a museum. That meeting's agenda may look like the one appearing in Exhibit 2.

As we shall see, the meeting leader's task will include completing the meeting's agenda in the allotted time. In the case of the agenda just outlined, the leader will need to keep the meeting hopping to complete all five items in one hour. But, as some famous principle says, work tends to expand to take up the time allowed. For instance, since one hour is allotted to this meeting, a good meeting leader will complete the meeting in 59 minutes or less. If two hours are allotted, a productive Ringmaster would make sure the meeting concludes within 119 minutes.

Exhibit 2. Agenda

Tuesday, June 11

10 A.M.—11 A.M.

1. Purpose of Meeting
2. Listing Local Wildlife Species
3. Planning Fund-raising Drive
4. Starting a Campaign to Recruit New Members
5. Wrap-up

Now, here it comes...the meeting is announced...the agenda is planned...now it is time to (listen to the drumroll)...actually *conduct* the meeting.

Step 3: Conduct the Meeting

For the Ringmaster, the actual conducting of each meeting is like jumping head first into the middle of a swimming pool. There is no choice. Either sink or swim.

Since few Ringmasters drown, it is a matter of how well a leader swims, that is, how productive the meeting is. That presents no problem to the astute Ringmaster who controls four meeting ingredients to his or her advantage:

1. Physical environment
2. Tone or atmosphere
3. Leader's role
4. Type of meeting

How to Create the Best Physical Environment for Your Meeting

Arranging the physical environment boils down to

1. Reserving a room of adequate size

2. Obtaining equipment, for exampl,e projectors and flip charts

3. Ordering refreshments, if desired, and making certain they are available when needed

4. Checking the seating arrangements, heating or air conditioning, and lighting *before* the meeting

5. Inspecting the equipment and making sure it functions *before* the meeting

6. If participants are unfamiliar with the meeting room location, making sure the room is easy to find

How to Create the Most Productive Meeting Tone

Once you tend to the physical environment, the Ringmaster must *create* the desired meeting atmosphere or tone. To do so, turn again to our trusty *4 Interpersonal Styles*. Here is how to set the atmosphere for meetings of each style:

1. *Results-Focused Meeting.* Such a meeting *quickly* zeros in on what time it is, not how to build a clock.

2. *Detail-Focused Meeting.* In sharp contrast to a results-focused meeting, a Detail-Focused meeting goes into excruciating nitty-gritty detail on how to build a clock.

3. *Friendly-Focused Meeting.* This type of meeting starts as a chummy, good cheer sort of get-together. Everyone smiles a lot, chats, and acts happy to be together. Then, after two to five minutes of friendly banter, the meeting usually reverts to a more results-focused or detail-focused tone.

4. *Partying-Focused Meeting.* Here, the initial focus is on having a grand time. Such meetings do not occur too often, because it is hard to get anything substantive

accomplished. An after-dinner meeting at a corporate retreat may be partying-focused. Some conventions are. If any real business is to be discussed, the leader first must let participants get some partying out of their systems, and then move toward a more results-focused or detail-focused style. Warning: A meeting leader who must keep a tight rein on a meeting to finish all agenda items on time should avoid letting a meeting get partying-focused.

How to Assume the Role of Leader

A meeting leader needs to juggle many balls at once. Success in keeping all the balls in the air results in a superbly productive meeting. Dropping any ball makes the leader look bad and could destroy the meeting's usefulness. Therefore, it is crucial for the leader to (1) know his or her own main purpose, (2) keep tabs on time, (3) take the right actions before starting the meeting, and (4) appeal to the participants' three main senses. Also, very important, the expert Ringmaster adeptly handles many types of personalities and smoothly encourages yet controls discussions.

In the beginning, the leader's main purpose is to set the meeting's tone and pace. Next, the leader must set the meeting's pace. Luckily, the Ringmaster can follow a simple guideline: Set whatever pace is needed to get the meeting finished at its stated ending time. To do so, Ringmasters always *start on time* and *end on time*. Period. That is it. It really is that simple.

To do so, successful Ringmasters employ the Hourglass Phenomenon. Quickly stated, the Hourglass Phenomenon means the leader keeps every meeting rolling along on time. There is nothing much to discuss about this phenomenon, which is a hard-and-fast rule at $99^{44}/_{100}\%$ of all meetings.

To make it work, the Ringmaster should frequently tell participants (1) how much time is left in the meeting and (2) how much of the agenda still needs to be completed. Such reminders every 10–20 minutes keep people plugging away to finish on time.

Even before the meeting starts, the leader has a small yet key job to do. The successful leader arrives early to greet participants. While this may seem minor, it actually accomplishes a much larger purpose. Specifically, most people crave attention. Someone greeting them provides the kind of attention most people like. Furthermore, to have the meeting's leader greet them shows attention plus respect; you are implicitly conveying that the meeting's participants are important. Also, after giving participants this extra bit of attention, they are more likely to feel positive toward you. Since a Ringmaster can use all the help he or she can muster, creating some good feelings can go a long way.

Well, let us imagine the meeting time arrives. What is the leader to do? Again, it is very straightforward. The leader must

1. Start the meeting on time.
2. Immediately state the meeting's main goal or desired end result.
3. Distribute the agenda or flash a transparency of it on a screen.
4. Then immediately review the agenda point by point.

Doing so in quick, rata-tat-tat order gets the meeting off to an organized start and shows that you mean business.

During the meeting, the leader needs to keep the meeting perking along at a good clip. To do so, a Ringmaster uses the participants' three key senses:

1. Auditory
2. Visual
3. Emotions

All meetings use participants' *auditory* sense, namely, people talk and hear. Better meetings involve the *visual* sense, too, by spicing up the meeting with transparencies, slides, handouts, flip charts, videos, or demonstrations. Going one giant step further requires using yet a third key sense—*emotions*. Dynamic meetings evoke good feelings, such as interest (at the very least), enjoyment, and fired-up motivation.

A winning meeting taps into the participants' auditory, visual, and emotional senses. It hits them in the ears, eyes, and heart. In sharp contrast, an insomnia-curing meeting generally taps into only one or two of these three senses and tends to leave a bad impression—after all, how many people would consider the leader of a boring meeting very dynamic? Not many.

Next, we come to an aspect of the leader's role that often sends shivers up a leader's spine: How do you handle all the different personalities that pop up in a meeting? The cooperative and enthusiastic ones are a joy, since they help the meeting flow smoothly and reach its goals.

However, other problem personalities will be found in practically every meeting. To handle these a Ringmaster needs the smooth skill and tact of a diplomat. There are four potentially troublesome types:

1. Silent One
2. Scarecrow
3. Motormouth
4. Arguer

The *Silent One* acts as if someone cut out his or her tongue. This type of person may be silent for a variety of reasons, but regardless of the reason, Silent Ones do not speak up in meetings. Since a good Ringmaster invites only those who truly (1) need to attend and (2) can add something of value to the proceedings, it is likely that Silent Ones *would* make worthwhile contributions, if only they *would* speak.

To tactfully handle Silent Ones,

✳ Call on the person to ask for input, or

✳ Give the person assignments such as reporting on important matters

A second troublesome participant in a meeting drama is the *Scarecrow*. This person is afraid to speak up, participate, and sometimes, even to sit in a meeting. Such a person may simply be shy. Oftentimes, this fearful behavior had its origins in a long-ago meeting during which the person was attacked and felt humiliated. The shock and hurt runs deep. So a Ringmaster must assume the role of a behavior therapist. To accomplish this, call on the person and then *immediately reinforce* the Scarecrow's input. It is also important not to allow anyone to attack the Scarecrow, since that would surely perpetuate the Scarecrow's worst fears. A sensitive, helpful Ringmaster plays a key role in bringing out what a Scarecrow has to offer.

The *Motormouth* feels he or she makes brilliant, witty, and creative contributions. Indeed, using this shotgun method of spewing forth loads of ideas, every so often Motormouth hits a target. Those bull's-eyes reinforce Motormouth, and keep the person charged up and wildly firing.

The Ringmaster must deal directly with this character, so as not to reinforce these actions. For instance, the Ringmaster may call on others or specifically ask questions for others to answer. If Motormouth speaks up, the meeting leader should matter-of-factly state, "You already have said a lot on this topic, so now we need to give others a chance to contribute" or words to that effect. Another tactic is for the Ringmaster to summarize what Motormouth said and then move on. Another excellent antidote is to point out the meeting's time limits and say, "We need to finish by such-and-such time. With so much talk now, we're going to have to rush to finish all our agenda items *on time*," and then continue.

Finally, there is the *Arguer*. If you say something is up, the Arguer insists it is down. If someone thinks something is a good idea, then the Arguer points out why it is an awful idea. The Arguer often considers himself clever, since he is so adept at pointing out how everyone else is wrong, inexact, stupid, naive, or less than intelligent. These actions make the Arguer not only bothersome, but also a roadblock to a smoothly run, productive meeting. The Arguer must be tackled—tactfully, of course.

To do this, the diplomatic Ringmaster avoids arguing with the Arguer. Doing so only makes the Ringmaster a participant in the Arguer's game.

If the Arguer continues making intrusive comments, the leader might look straight into the eyes of the Arguer and point out the Arguer's repeated behaviors.

Often, meeting participants feel too embarrassed or scared to say anything to the Arguer about how his or her actions impact them. So, it is up to the Ringmaster to do so. For example, the Ringmaster might say to the Arguer, "It seems like practically every time someone says something, you argue with it. Sometimes your remarks seem right on target. Sometimes, however, your comments tend to promote more conflict than cooperation. In addition, your arguing may inhibit others from speaking up, because they feel you put them down. That may not be your intention, but that is how your arguing can affect our meeting."

If the Arguer then argues with this statement, the Ringmaster can reply, "You're still doing it. You couldn't resist arguing with me. Now, let's continue and *get some results* from this meeting before our time is up."

How to Encourage and Control Participation

In addition to handling many and varied types of personalities, the Ringmaster also needs to encourage and control audience participation.

This usually is easy. After all, only people who have something to contribute are invited to a good meeting. Given this fact, the Ringmaster can encourage participation in several ways. Easiest of all is just to let people talk. To do this, the leader cannot become so enamored with his or her own voice that the leader does not let others get a word in edgewise. Also, the Ringmaster should reinforce others' participation with compliments, acknowledgments, and shows of appreciation. The leader can request discussion. By asking open-ended questions, such as, "What do all of you think about that?" or "What course of action might we take?" the leader can elicit responses. Additionally, at its most basic, the leader can start the meeting by stating that one "ground rule" is that attendees must participate in the discussions.

While encouraging audience participation often is a piece of cake, *controlling audience participation* may cause some sparks to fly, unless it is done with tact and diplomacy. To do this, the meeting leader *always* must keep control of the meeting. Or, put another way, the meeting leader must *never lose control of the meeting*. The leader is the person in charge. Even when the meeting ventures into brainstorming, free-for-all discussions or other creative participation, the Ringmaster always must maintain control over the event.

Problems can arise if a participant tries to take control of the meeting. For example, a participant may hog the floor, talk excessively, or try to make the meeting's discussion revolve around him or her. When such antics occur, the leader must assess if the meeting will reach its initial goals. If the answer is negative, then the leader must take control of the meeting. There are a handful of generally effective methods for doing this. For instance, the leader could stand. This tactic is effective, because typically the person whose head is highest in a room controls the room. If the person trying to seize control is standing while the leader is sitting, the leader should stand. Height creates power.

Once while chairing a symposium at a business conference, I sat down while the symposium panel members and I fielded questions from the audience. One audience member stood up and proceeded to plug his firm's product while ostensibly asking a question. With one question answered, the audience member proceeded to ask another, again making a rambling pitch for his firm's product.

Suddenly, I realized what was happening. That audience member was hogging the floor and taking control of the meeting. I also realized he was standing while everyone else in the room, including me, sat. So, I stood up. Immediately, he slowed his talking and glared at me as if he sensed a challenge to his turf. When he paused for a breath, I seized the opportunity to speak. I explained, "We need to move on to another questioner." In doing so, I regained control of the meeting and was able to keep it moving along.

Another way to regain control of a meeting is with an overhead transparency projector if one is already being used. Flip it on or off to get attention and regain control. If the projector is off, then flip it on to show a transparency. The best transparency may be the one that shows the meeting's agenda. With that on the screen, point out that "finishing our agenda on time requires that we move along right now."

Interestingly, a stuffed-shirt parliamentarian approach often works wonders: Stop others from controlling a meeting by stating, "I'm exercising the prerogative of the chair by moving us along through the agenda." The formality of this approach catches participants by surprise, and the statement is usually followed by a few seconds of silence, which allows the Ringmaster to regain control.

Finally, the most direct approach is simply to *set time limits*. Just tell participants that to finish on time the meeting must continue right now. This is very simple, and it really works well. Few participants want to seem like they do not care about finishing on time. As such, the Ringmaster announces time limits to reassert his or her control of the meeting.

How to Smoothly Lead the Three Types of Meetings

There are three main types of meetings

1. Informative
2. Persuasive
3. Planning and problem solving

A successful business or professional person leads all three equally well.

Easiest of all is the *informative* meeting. Here, the Ringmaster merely starts on time, states the meeting's purpose, and follows the agenda. Information, such as progress reports or data, is conveyed. Questions are answered. Relevant topics are discussed. Tasks are assigned. Also, importantly, the meeting ends on time.

Persuasive meetings start like informative ones. They begin on time, with the Ringmaster reviewing the meeting's goal and agenda. After that, leading the meeting takes a particular twist. First, the leader states the opposition's viewpoint, and then asks the opposing side for its input. Why is the opposing side accorded such time and respect? Simple. People love it when others *show* that their viewpoints are important and understood. Also, people hate feeling ignored or not having their viewpoint aired. Thus, getting the opposing side's viewpoint out on the table and respected is the first major order of business. When that is done, state your viewpoint. Negotiation follows. Then, the meeting's final decisions should be stated so everyone hears a clear description of what was decided. The persuasive meeting ends on time, of course.

Here's an example of how such a persuasive meeting might go: An executive wanted to save some money on a production project. However, the manager in charge of the project knew that a higher quality and more salable product would result if certain more expensive components were used. So the project manager called a meeting with the executive and others on the production team. The meeting started on time. The stated goal was to decide how to proceed with the project. The agenda consisted of reviewing the alternatives, especially the executive's ideas and the project manager's ideas, and then reaching an agreement. At this point, the project manager could have ranted and raved about her ideas, or she could get the executive's ideas out on the table.

She chose the latter approach, and kicked off the discussion by asking the executive, "What are your thoughts about carrying out this project?" The executive detailed his ideas. Then, the project manager summarized the executive's ideas and pointed out how those ideas seemed really good and useful. By this time, the executive felt he had been listened to, understood, respected for his ideas, and in an important sense, appreciated.

With rapport established, the stage was set. The project's manager launched into her proposal for the project. She diplomatically compared and contrasted the likely success of the project under both the executive's scenario and her own. Upon fully hearing out the project manager, and negotiating a bit, the executive agreed the manager's approach would turn out better than his.

As a result of taking this approach, the executive changed his views, approved another's ideas, and actually left feeling good about the outcome—even though the project would not proceed according to the plan he initially favored. This accomplished, the Ringmaster cemented her success in this persuasive meeting by summarizing the final negotiated action plan for carrying out the project. The meeting ended on time.

So far, the informative meeting and the persuasive meeting have been discussed. One more meeting type exists in professional and business circles; that is, the extraordinarily important *planning and problem-solving* meeting. A huge number of crucial meetings are of this type. Their goals range from deciding how to organize an event to devising long-term organizational strategy, from determining the best patient treatment method for a tricky case to banging out a monstrous agreement. Planning and problem-solving meetings can produce tremendous benefits. (Indeed, each day meetings that cost $5,000 to hold produce million-dollar results. That certainly looks like a magnificent investment.)

Good Ringmasters run planning and problem-solving meetings very much as they would other types of meetings. The meeting begins on time, the Ringmaster clearly describes the meeting's goals, and a well-laid-out agenda is followed. Flip charts or chalkboards are used to write, for all to see, major points and ideas generated during the meeting. Quite often the Ringmaster orchestrates the meeting using group problem-solving techniques, such as brainstorming, open discussion, cause-and-effect analysis, and other such methods. After the problem-solving and planning, the Ringmaster assigns tasks for participants to complete following the meeting. To conclude, the meeting leader

1. Summarizes the meeting accomplishments
2. Ends the meeting on time

This concludes how to conduct the three major types of meetings. Each possesses much in common, and a superb Ringmaster conducts each with ease and agility. The Ringmaster always stays in control of what goes on, makes certain the meetings always start and end on time, uses a written agenda, and ensures that participants accomplish the meeting's stated goals.

Such well-run meetings produce impressive benefits for professionals and businesspeople, as well as for their organizations, clients, customers, and patients. A key reason for this success is the thought emblazoned across every fine Ringmaster's forehead: *The Meter Always Is Ticking.*

Step 4: Conclude the Meeting

Breaking up a meeting is not hard to do. It boils down to a small number of steps. The skillful Ringmaster devoutly follows these steps. The less-skilled meeting leader does not realize until too late that he or she must take specific actions to conclude a meeting.

First, the Ringmaster summarizes the meeting's accomplishments. He or she clearly and concisely states how the meeting met its initial goals.

Then, the agile meeting leader clearly and in no uncertain terms describes the agreed-upon actions participants must perform if there is to be successful follow through. The leader states the

1. Actions to be taken

2. Person assigned to follow up on each action

3. Date on which each action should be completed

4. Next step to be taken after completing each action, for example, the need to convey information via memos, reports, or follow-up meetings

For example, a Ringmaster may state something like "Victoria and Jennifer agreed to complete the marketing study by the last day in October. Included in their study will be a detailed action plan outlining (1) precisely what products we should sell, (2) the size of the likely market, and (3) pricing guidelines, along with (4) a sample salesperson's package to be used to sell the new products. When this is completed, Victoria and Jennifer will call another meeting of this group to announce their marketing plan and figure out exactly how to put it into action. That meeting will take place on November 10."

Step 5: Post-meeting Follow-up

Earlier in this chapter, we saw how, for the Ringmaster, meetings begin *before* they actually occur. That is because before a meeting a skilled meeting leader devises the meeting's goals, invites appropriate participants, creates the agenda, and makes plans to hold the meeting. And, as with planning a meeting,

Be Aware and Beware:
Your meeting is NOT over even after it is over.

After the meeting, the Ringmaster still has important things to do. For example, the leader needs to ask participants for feedback, such as "How did the meeting go for you?" or "What are your thoughts about the meeting?" Such feedback-seeking questions accomplish two goals. First, participants give the Ringmaster ideas of what went well so he or she can repeat those things in the future. Also, the Ringmaster unearths ideas for how to lead even more productive meetings.

Second, the Ringmaster further establishes himself or herself as someone who really cares about the participants' thoughts, needs, feelings, and reactions. Doing so helps the Ringmaster start future meetings with cared-for participants even more gung-ho on helping the Ringmaster conduct a highly productive meeting.

It is also sometimes helpful for the Ringmaster to write follow-up memos or letters to

* Summarize the meeting's accomplishments
* Schedule further meetings
* Personally contact participants who are carrying out assignments made in the meeting

CHECKLIST—
HOW TO CONDUCT HIGHLY PRODUCTIVE
MEETINGS

_____ Remember the bottom line—"The meter always is ticking"

_____ Plan meeting

_____ Announce goals

_____ Circulate announcement memo, if needed

_____ Organize agenda

_____ Conduct meeting

_____ Ensure optimal physical environment

_____ Start on time

_____ Create productive meeting tone

_____ Finish all agenda items within allotted time

_____ End on time

_____ Conclude meeting

_____ Summarize decisions

_____ Summarize assignments participants must do

_____ Follow up after meeting

HOW TO DEVELOP BUSINESS WRITING SKILLS*

HOW TO WRITE CRISP, CLEAR MEMOS, LETTERS, AND REPORTS QUICKLY

The sixth most important high-impact communications skill zeros in on a skill many humans consider bothersome, hard, an annoying pain, and anxiety provoking, namely, writing. Far too many people dread writing. It often causes the faint-of-heart to flee and the stronger ones to sweat bullets.

Fortunately, though, mastering a fairly small number of techniques empowers anyone to write with ease, grace, clarity, speed and—yes!—even enjoyment.

This chapter

* Uncovers the breathtaking costs of business writing

* Provides a no-nonsense guideline for what good business writing is

*The author thanks his sister Meridith for all she taught him about effective writing skills.

✳ Lays bare the secret of how to appeal to, and win over, your readers

✳ Describes a scientifically proven method that simultaneously speeds up writing and makes writing more enjoyable

✳ Tells how to use the foregoing points in combination with other high-impact people skills to dash off amazingly well-written informative or persuasive memos, letters, and reports

Do You Realize How Very Expensive Business Writing Really Is?

The typical business letter costs over $16 to write, according to a Midwestern company that researched such costs. A large New York–based consumer products company found its average middle manager *wasted* $3,187 yearly creating unusable memos, letters, and reports. The money washed down the drain included discarded writing, procrastination time, and secretarial typing and retyping services. A chunk of change this size is nothing to sneeze at.

Think about it. Better yet, quickly calculate how much money *you* waste on unusable writing, using the following steps to compute your loss.

How Much Money *You* Waste on Useless Memos, Letters, and Reports

Step	What to Calculate	Amount of Money
1	How much are you paid, or could you earn, per hour?	$_____
2	What is 50% of the amount you wrote in step 1? This amount	

	pays for your benefits, office costs, and other expenses. (Step 1 × 0.50 = $_____)	$_____
3	Add steps 1 and 2 to determine how much you really cost per hour.	$_____
4	Multiply the amount in step 3 by the number of hours you waste annually on writing unusable memos, letters, and reports.	
	Or, if it is easier, multiply the number of hours you wasted last week times 50 weeks (or however many weeks you work annually).	$_____
5	Calculate secretarial wages and benefits per hour and multiply that number by the number of hours a secretary wastes typing and retyping your unusable writing.	$_____
6	Add steps 4 and 5 to get the total amount of money you wasted.	$_____
7	Gasp at how much money you *waste* on unusable writing per year.	

The dollar amount you wasted does not even reflect the money wasted by people who need to decipher the unclear writing you sent them. You, in effect, forced them to squander their dollars, as well as their time, energy, and patience with you.

Doing these calculations quantifies the financial imperative to write quickly and well, not to mention the toll writing takes on your nerves.

Why Do So Many People Hate to Write?

Children in kindergarten and beginning first grade absolutely love to write. Writing feels like a game or toy to them. It is fun. These findings popped up in a ground-breaking University of New Hampshire research study cited later in this chapter.

Unfortunately, many teachers actually *teach children to hate to write.* Note: Few grade school or high school instructors ever teach either how to write well or how to enjoy writing. Instead, teachers often create fear and dread of writing.

How does this happen? Easily, very easily. Teachers simply uncap their *red* pens to mark up and criticize the writing students turn in to them. These all-too-typical experiences snowball over the years until writing for many adults subconsciously means getting stung with humiliating red marks. It fuels a dread of writing.

In addition, such a criticism-oriented approach washes away the glee children naturally feel when they express themselves. Those teachers who perpetuate this ego-deflating process create an Alice-in-Wonderland sense which only the most clear-sighted can see through.[1]

All in all, many people dread writing because to them writing signals an attack on their self-respect, self-worth, and self-esteem. Fortunately, everyone can overcome these dreads. It just takes learning how to write quickly, easily, and

---

[1]This sentence ended with a preposition ("through") that many teachers would say is incorrect. Too many such lapses result in loads of red marks scrawled across homework papers.

Actually, I like how Winston Churchill handled this. He once wrote a speech and allowed someone to read it before he delivered it. At one place on the manuscript, the reader jotted a note to Churchill indicating that the prime minister ended a sentence with a preposition. Upon seeing this criticism, Churchill replied, "That is the sort of criticism up with which I shall not put!"

well. That is exactly what this chapter lays out for *your immediate use.*

HOW TO MAKE YOUR BUSINESS WRITING *LOOK* LIKE A WINNER

Everyone wants to write well. But what does good business writing look like?

Here goes. Impressive memos, letters, and reports contain

* *Clear, easy-to-understand* phrases, sentences, paragraphs, and subtitles
* *Easy-to-follow, logical* ideas, facts, and reasoning
* *Good spelling and grammar*
* A *focus on the reader's needs*, not on the writer's needs
* Some *lively, colorful words and phrases*
* *Consistent, easy-to-read format*

Following this chapter's pointers can result in you doing such top-notch writing.

The First Step Toward Good Writing: "Read" Your Reader's Needs and Desires

Writing begins before you scrawl any words across a piece of paper. It starts by pinpointing your eventual reader's personality and needs and, given those, determining how to please that reader.

Why bother? Because business writing aims to fulfill the *reader's needs*, and not the writer's needs. The reader needs to be informed or persuaded, not the writer. To accomplish this, writing must come across as reader oriented, not writer oriented: *Thee* proves vastly more important in writing than *me*.

To do this, reflect on where your reader falls in the *4 Interpersonal Styles*. As described in other chapters, this method divides people into four fairly readily spotted types:

1. Results-focused
2. Detail-focused
3. Friendly-focused
4. Partying-focused

The reader's primary focus bears great weight in deciding how to appeal to him or her. For instance, a Results-Focused reader mainly wants to know what time it is, while a Detail-Focused reader craves the entire story about how you built a clock. A Friendly-Focused reader wants writing that comes across as personal, writing that pays special attention to the reader's likes, dislikes, feelings, and lifestyle. Finally, a Partying-Focused reader demands writing that is fun, weaving in a joke or two, some tongue-in-cheek remarks, and upbeat references.

As an example, let's look at how to express the same idea to people in each of the four groups.

Memo to a Results-Focused Reader

As we discussed, we will meet from 3 to 4 P.M. on Tuesday in the main conference room to discuss ways to improve your staff's writing skills.

Memo to a Detail-Focused Reader

This memo recaps our discussion we held on Friday afternoon, June 14. As you recall, that was our third discussion about how to improve your department's writing skills. During our June 14 discussion, we focused on four writing skills that your staff needs to improve. They are

1. Writing faster
2. Writing more clearly
3. Adopting more reader orientation and less writer orientation
4. Improving formatting neatness

To plan how to train your department's employees in these skills, let's meet from 3 to 4 P.M. on Tuesday, June 25, in the main conference room.

At our meeting, we will

1. Review your staff's writing problems
2. Pinpoint the specific writing problems shown by *each* employee in your department
3. Decide on a timetable for providing writing skills training
4. Schedule each employee for his or her needed writing skills training

Thank you. We'll talk in more detail at our June 25 meeting, from 3 to 4 P.M.

to a Friendly-Focused Reader

I greatly enjoyed getting together with you last Friday. We certainly covered a lot of ground together. It fascinates me to see how very much your department's writing problems mirror the problems my department used to have.

That probably makes you all the more confident we can help your staff. After all, if my department can improve so quickly on these crucial skills, then your department probably can get equally fast, dramatic results.

Let's get together to discuss how we can collaborate on Tuesday, June 25, from 3 to 4 P.M. in the main conference room. We'll jointly plan exactly how to overcome the problems. That would lift a big burden off your shoulders.

I'm looking forward to seeing you Tuesday.

to a Partying-Focused Reader

You *always* crack me up!! It never fails to amaze me. When you showed me examples of your staff's memos, letters and reports, I thought I would bust a gut from laughing so hard. I cannot remember the last time I saw such hilarious excuses for business writing.

Well, we must do something to get your staff's writing skills up to par. Let's decide what to do by meeting on Tuesday, June 25, from 3 to 4 P.M., in the main conference room.

If you dig up any more humorous writing examples, please make sure you bring them to show me. I can barely wait.

Another consideration centers on using *reader-oriented language*. Rule:

> Use the reader's terms and language,
> regardless how you (the writer) normally speak.

For instance, an accountant may refer to "accounts receivable." However, the accountant should avoid writing to a nonfinancially oriented client, "Our accounts receivable records show a $3,187 debit on your account." Instead, the accountant simply should write, "You owe $3,187." The message remains the same. However, the message is much easier for the reader to grasp when it appears in the reader's language, not the writer's language.

HOW TO WRITE FASTER AND BETTER (PLUS ENJOY IT MORE)

Most people prefer to avoid writing if at all possible. Writing pains them. They doubt their ability. These common feelings may have reached epidemic proportions. They hamper productivity, happiness, and self-esteem and eliminate a crucial communications medium.

To find out how to overcome this epidemic, the University of New Hampshire conducted a major scientific study of how to teach business writing skills so people learn to write

* better
* quicker
* more enjoyably

The research findings offer a dramatic breakthrough on how to improve writing skill and speed.

Specifically, the results indicate the best way to write well is *freewriting*. To use freewriting, a person simply does these three steps *one at a time*:

1. *Outline.* The more detailed the outline, the easier step 2 will be.

2. *Write*. Transform your outline into sentences and paragraphs.

3. *Edit*. Spruce up what you wrote in step 2.

It is very important to *avoid combining any of the three steps*. However, when most people write, they do two or three of the steps simultaneously. That provides a great opportunity to trip over your own feet. While it would seem that doing two or three steps simultaneously would save time, it actually takes more time. It also helps procrastinators dawdle and waste even more time.

Also, I consistently find that the more detailed the outline (step 1), the easier and faster my writing (step 2) proceeds. Most people experience the same thing. So it pays to create a *detailed outline*. If you find your writing (step 2) takes longer than you like or does not flow smoothly, then you probably did not make an adequately detailed outline. So, next time, make a more detailed outline *before* you transform your words of wisdom into sentences and paragraphs.

EVERYTHING YOU ALWAYS WANTED TO KNOW ABOUT HOW TO WRITE LIKE A WINNER

An awful lot of people suspect good writing is a matter of upbringing, luck, or mysterious hocus-pocus. Little could be farther from the truth. Indeed, good writing proves totally learnable and teachable. Of course, too many writing teachers wrap up writing skills in a shroud of unneeded, hard-to-use, and even harder-to-recall techniques.

Instead, *writing well boils down to only nine main techniques*. As presented here, these techniques slice through the fluff and pomp of most writing instruction to get straight to the essentials you need.

Technique 1: Speeded Up Outlining

Architects and business planners both use a similar phrase: *Form follows function.* It means that first a person must decide what outcome or goal you want to accomplish. Then, the person can devise the exact form the outline must take. For instance, an architect first must find out what purposes (function) a building will serve, and then the architect can design the building (form). For example, a building containing a 1,000-seat auditorium needs a different form than a building meant to house 100 small offices. Form follows function.

The same is true for the business or professional person who must write. In writing, the first step involves creating an outline of the main points your memo, letter, or report must cover.

Forget about the classy Roman numeral type of outline you learned school. You could use it if you're comfortable with it. However, you seldom require such a fancy outline. Instead, your outline can merely include the

* Big points you plan to cover
* Brief notes to yourself mentioning what to say about each big point

For example, I created the outline shown below to write this chapter up to this point.

Outline Used to Write First Part of This Chapter

---

1. Introduction
2. High Cost of Business Writing
   a. Studies/research
   b. Calculations

3. Why People Dread Writing
   a. Teachers
   b. Red ink
   c. Fears
   d. Suggestions
4. How Does Good Business Writing Look
   a. Clear
   b. Logical
   c. Spelling, grammar, punctuation
   d. Reader's needs, not writer's needs
   e. Lively, colorful phrasing
5. Step 1: "Read" Readers
   a. Reader-oriented 4 *Interpersonal Styles*
   b. Reader's needs, not writer's needs
   c. Reader's language, not writer's language
6. How to Enjoy Writing Faster, Better
   a. University of New Hampshire study
   b. Freewriting .
7. Everything You Always Wanted to Know About How to Write Well...

After creating an outline, the writer only has to go through the outline point by point, converting each point into a sentence or paragraph. The writer explains one point, then proceeds to the next point, and then the next point, and so on until the writer finishes the entire outline.

Fortunately, outlining is rather simple, creative, and fun to do. You can do it on writing paper, on your computer, or on the backs of napkins. For example, I've outlined each book and article I ever wrote on napkins and paper placemats in restaurants. Somehow, that is where my creative juices flow best.

Technique 2: K.I.S.S. Your Reader

High-achievers and positive thinkers define K.I.S.S. as *K*eep *I*t *S*hort and *S*imple. Winningly K.I.S.S. your reader in three closely linked ways.

1. *Use Short Words.* For instance, write "think" rather than "contemplate" and "use" rather than "utilize." Grab a thesaurus or dictionary to fight long-word mania. Look at the following list for more examples of easily replaceable words.

Long Words and Their Short-Word Equals

Long Word	Short Word
approximately	about, around
ascertain	learn
calculate	figure
compensation	pay, wages, salary
concerning	about
contemplate	think
demonstrate	show
disseminate	send
expenditure	cost
implement (verb)	do
implement (noun)	tool
initiate	start, begin
monitor	check
optimum	best, tops, finest

per annum	yearly, annually
presently	now
proposition	offer
reimbursement	repay, pay back
subsequent	next
terminate	end, fire
utilize	use

Sometimes after I recommend that people use short words, they give me examples of long words that mean something special in their company or industry *and* are hard to replace with a shorter one. They also cite some long words they absolutely love using. If there are long words you must use or love using, go ahead and use them, but remember, in all other cases, when possible, use short words. Your readers will appreciate it.

2. *Use Short Sentences.* Short sentences are easier to read than long sentences. In general, keep your sentences to

   ✳ about 15 words or less

   ✳ two or fewer typed lines

3. *Avoid Fog.* Fog refers to how much deep thought a reader must use to figure out what a writer means. Reading foggy writing feels like swimming in a pool filled with gelatin. To avoid such problems, use short words in short sentences, and to keep fog to a minimum.

Technique 3: Vibrate with Vibrant Words

Vibrant, *active* wording captures your reader's attention, hooks him, and keeps him involved. In contrast, more passive phrasing comes across as less vibrant.

Throughout high school, college, and graduate school, I heard instructors say, "Use active verbs and avoid passive verbs." I never knew what they meant.

When I finished graduate school and entered the work force, I attended a number of business writing workshops. In each, the trainer told us, "Use active verbs, avoid passive verbs." It was the same phrase I heard in school. It reminded me of Yogi Berra's observation, "It's like *déjà vu* all over again."

However, I still did not understand the difference between active and passive verbs. Each time I asked an instructor or corporate trainer, I always heard the same answer, "Active verbs are active, and passive verbs are passive." That certainly provided no help to me.

Finally, I asked an instructor to write some sentences using passive verbs, along with equivalent sentences using active verbs. As I examined these two lists, a pattern emerged. I realized that passive verbs all employed variations of the verb "be." Active verbs did not.

So here is the easiest and quickest way I have ever seen to make sure you "Use active verbs and avoid using passive verbs." It's simple. Just avoid using the verbs shown here:

Passive Verbs to Avoid

be	is	are	was	were
–	has	have	had	have had
been	has been	have been	had been	–

And make your writing shine by using lots of *vibrantly active verbs*, such as those that follow:

Vibrant, Active Verbs to Use in Your Memos, Letters, and Reports

---

anticipate	increase
avoid	innovate
catalyze	jump
create	kick
decrease	launch
develop	pinpoint
do	prove
elevate	reduce
enhance	save
excite	spot
flow	start
generate	state
give glow	tell
identify	thrill
impact	

Another way to make your writing appear more lively is to use *vibrant adjectives and adverbs* like these:

Colorful Adjectives and Adverbs to Add Spice to Your Writing

amazing	long-range
authoritative	moderately
custom-tailored	on-target
dreary	outstanding
dynamic	potential
effective	practical
elegant	pragmatic
excellent	quickly
exquisite	sharp
extremely	simply
grand	spectacular
great	stately
handsomely	successful
handy	superb
immediate	tested
incredible	top-notch
instantly	tremendous
limited	vast

Crisp, clear, intriguing business writing requires phrasing loaded with activity. Yet most people seem vastly more adept at crafting passive phrases than active phrases. The table on below demonstrates how to convert passive phrases into active phrases just by

* throwing away the passive verbs
* inserting active verbs
* rearranging the sentence, when necessary

Easily Converting Passive Phrases into Active Phrases

Passive Phrases	*Active Phrases*
I <u>am</u> excited.	I feel excited.
He <u>was</u> enthusiastic.	He oozed enthusiasm.
I <u>am</u> thrilled with your accomplishments.	Your accomplishments thrill me.
They <u>have been</u> pleased.	It pleased them.
The movie <u>has been</u> enjoyable to us.	We enjoyed the movie.
Mr. James <u>was</u> late getting back from the bank.	Mr. James returned late from the bank.
He <u>has</u> said he liked that.	He said he liked that.

Note: Each passive verb is underlined. See page 177 for a complete list of passive verbs to avoid.

Technique 4: Add Color with Choice Words and Phrases

A leading women's clothing executive described a fashion show by writing about the "exquisitely outfitted, regal procession of mannequins." She could just as easily have stated, "The nicely dressed models walked down the runway." However, she chose a delightfully more image-filled, magnetic word feast to say the same thing.

Other examples come from a corporate information systems executive. In his monthly report on computer service levels, he makes blazing points, such as

* ✳ "The Order Entry Department achieved 97%, exceeding our goal and a substantial improvement over last month."
* ✳ "Inventory Control Department hit 100%, an outstanding month."

This executive's written remarks would seem vastly less colorful if he wrote the same ideas like this:

* ✳ "The Order Entry Department had a 97% service level fulfillment."
* ✳ "The Inventory Control Department met all its service levels."

Instead of dull language, the executive used vibrant verbs (*achieved* and *hit*) followed by well-deserved brags (a *substantial improvement* and *an outstanding month*). Notice how just a few colorful, vibrant, somewhat flashy words turn a potentially lifeless topic (monthly computer service levels) into a lively foray into his group's accomplishments—a quality that makes this executive stand out as special. Colorful phrasing can inject life into practically any topic.

Look at the list of phrases that follows. It dramatically contrasts bland phrases with colorful ones. The bland phrases are simply descriptive. In contrast, the colorful phrases convey the same ideas with spice and vividness.

Bland Phrasing Versus Colorful Phrasing

Bland Phrases	*Colorful Phrases*
a good month	an outstanding month
many items	a vast array
boring brochure	dreary brochure
good food	luscious cuisine
very fine employee	top-notch performer
quite useful	wonderfully practical
quite interesting event	amazing phenomenon

I should point out that colorful phrasing often requires the use of long words. This could add to your writing "fog" count. Keep this in mind as you write.

To sum up, as you write, remember to (1) use short words and sentences as much as possible and (2) every once in awhile inject a colorful phrase to enliven your writing.

Technique 5: Plug in Words That Focus on Your Reader's Needs

Reader's needs must serve as the focal point of memos, letters, and reports. To do so, certain words can work some very special magic, namely,

✽ Use your reader's name.

❋ Throw in words showing your reader "owns" the topic of the writing. These words include "you," "your," "we," and "our." Such words mean a lot to your reader who craves to feel like a memo, letter, or report aims to fill his or her needs, and not just your (the writer's) needs.

The sample memo on page below demonstrates the use of a reader's own words. In the sample, these words are underlined, although they would not be in the actual memo.

Sample Memo:
Words That Focus on Reader's Needs

To: Terry Sample

From: Michael Mercer

Terry, you asked me to give you pointers on your writing skills. You especially wanted to know how you could help your readers feel more personally involved in the memos and letters you write.

Two powerful, easy-to-use methods exist at your fingertips:

1. Sprinkle your reader's name throughout your writing. For example, you could write, "Lee, thank you for your suggestion." Or you could write, "Thank you for your suggestion." The fact that you plug Lee's name into the phrase should get his attention. He definitely would notice and enjoy seeing his name in print, and as a result, he will probably pay closer attention to your message to him.

2. Plug key reader "ownership" words into your memos and letters. You and I and everyone else in the world love to shower attention on something we own. In contrast, we feel much more neutral about a topic we do not feel we "own." Fortunately, you hold the power to make your reader "own"

what <u>you</u> write and, therefore, feel it is of greater personal importance. For example, <u>you</u> could write, "The suggestion proved useful." or "<u>Your</u> suggestion proved useful." Both sentences convey the same basic idea, but the word "<u>your</u>" pulls in <u>your</u> reader more than "the."

<u>Terry</u>, I hope these two pointers help <u>you</u> the next time <u>you</u> write a memo or letter. Please let me know if I can help <u>you</u> in any other way.

Technique 6: P.S.: A Great Attention-Getter

People read the "P.S." at the end of a letter. Use this to your advantage. Every once in awhile, insert a "P.S." at the end of a letter stating a vital point you definitely want your reader to notice. Since people find it hard to resist reading the "P.S.," your point should get across.

P.S. Remember to do this!

Technique 7: Underline—It Eases Your Reader's Job...and Yours

<u>Read only the underlined phrases in the following para-graphs.</u>

A long stretch of type looks boringly like an eerie gray cloud floating close to the page's surface. Only the most devoutly Detail-Focused person enjoys reading a long stretch of uninterrupted type. Because of such masses of verbiage, <u>a lot of well-thought-out writing probably never gets read</u>. Busy professionals and businesspeople simply possess neither the time nor the patience to read pages of undifferentiated grayness. Doing so, the reader may feel, is too time consuming.

The <u>solution: Underline key words, ideas, or phrases</u>. It is that simple. Rather than force readers to grope through a cloudburst of words to find key points, help them. <u>Underline the most important points</u>. People who need or want to soak up the itsy-bitsy, teeny-weeny details can read everything you wrote. Everyone else (comfortably) <u>can read just the underlined parts</u> to grasp the essentials. Then, if they want, they can drift through the rest to reap the surrounding pearls of wisdom in all their magnificent glory.

Readers love writers who make things easy for them. <u>Underlining helps pave the way to being understood—fast</u>. In fact, for many ultra-busy readers, special features such as underlining govern whether or not they read what you write at all.

Technique 8: Add Clarity with Subtitles

The words immediately above are a subtitle or subheading. A subtitle tells the reader what point the writer is going to make. They are like road signs indicating directions or upcoming landmarks. A well-written memo, letter, or report should contain subheadings, especially if the memo, letter, or report is longer than one page. Subtitles are easy to create: They usually are a point you made while outlining the piece (see step 1 of *freewriting*, earlier in this chapter).

Most important, subheadings make your reader's job easy. For instance, a reader could open up to this chapter in the book and immediately thumb through the chapter looking for subtitles that catch his or her fancy. Then, the reader can read only those sections dealing with subjects that arouse his or her interest. Material following other subheadings could be passed over, skimmed, or read later.

Readers love writers who are easy to follow. Subtitles break any memo, letter or report into bite-size pieces. They are, you might say, fast and easy to digest. That makes subheadings a superbly potent, easy-to-use writing technique, indeed.

Technique 9: Benefit from Bullets—As Easy as 1-2-3

The following material is expressed in three different ways. Read each of these 3 examples and then select the one you find easiest *and* quickest to follow.

Example A

This chapter presents the points a writer needs to follow to write impressive letters, memos, and reports. Some skills covered include outlining, how to write quickly and enjoyably, the K.I.S.S. principle—why it proves important to Keep It Short and Simple, and how to spot and use vibrant verbs and colorful phrases.

Example B

Writing skills presented in this chapter include how to

- Outline
- Write quickly
- Enjoy writing
- K.I.S.S.—Keep It Short and Simple
- Use vibrant verbs and colorful phrasing

Example C

Writing skills presented in this chapter include how to

1. Outline
2. Write quickly
3. Enjoy writing
4. K.I.S.S.—Keep It Short and Simple
5. Use vibrant verbs and colorful phrases

Most readers say that Examples B and C prove much easier and quicker to read and understand than Example A. Reason: The use of bullets (•) or numbering of points conspicuously eases

1. Writing
2. Reading
3. Understanding
4. Finding the key points in any letter, memo, or report

Technique 10: Create Visual Impact

The most brilliantly composed report, letter, or memo loses its glitter if it doesn't look sharp on the typed page. If you work in an organization, you may want to examine the president's or chief executive's writing. It will demonstrate the organization's preferred format, and it may be wise for you to follow it.

Computer programs for word processing and desktop publishing and great printers make it easy to produce writing that looks sharp. Yet, even the best printing makes a poor impression unless certain essential guidelines are followed:

1. *Be consistent.* This includes using a consistent approach to

    a. spacing (single and double)
    b. paragraphs
    c. indentations
    d. subtitles
    e. page number placement[2]

---

[2]It always amazes me how many people do not realize it is contrary to tradition to put a page number on the first page of a memo, letter, or report. That is one of those little things that says a lot about a person's level of concern for professionalism. While this may seem picky, it does make a difference to many people who may judge you partly on how professional your writing looks at first glance.

2. *Check your spelling, grammar, and punctuation.* Anything less makes you look unprofessional, uneducated, sloppy, unconcerned, or all four. Mistakes on such matters make an instant impact on many readers, including people who could make or break your career.

3. *Create realistic margins.* This typically means an inch on all four sides of the page. If you plan to bind the material, then a 1.5-inch margin along the left side usually leaves enough space to do so.

HOW TO EXCEL AT THE 2 TYPES OF BUSINESS WRITING

There are two types of writing: (1) informative and (2) persuasive. If those sound familiar to you, it is because they are also the two main types of presentations. They also are two of the three types of meetings. These similarities are only fitting, since writing, speaking to groups, and leading meetings are all communications skills. The following guidelines will help you write informative and persuasive memos, letters, and reports that make you sound like a winner.

Informative Writing Techniques

Informative writing aims to convey information, facts, data, or how-to-do-it ideas. It demands that you get the information down in the simplest-to-digest manner possible.

As stated earlier, you must always write to meet your reader's needs, not your needs. The key concern here is whether or not the reader finds your writing easy to understand and interesting. Use all the writing techniques presented so far in this chapter to craft clear, crisp informative memos, letters, and reports.

Persuasive Writing Techniques

While informative writing is pretty straightforward and can be accomplished successfully by using the methods explained in this chapter, persuasive writing requires a few extra talents. Superbly crafted persuasive memos, letters, or reports sway readers' opinions, ideas, and actions.

5-Step Persuasive Writing Technique

You can reap the tremendous rewards of persuasive writing by mastering this simple technique.

First, start by diving into an overview of your *reader's needs*. Do not begin with your needs as the writer. Appeal to your reader's desire to

* Succeed
* Do well
* Stand out
* Achieve something of value

Second, after delving into your reader's needs, *pace your reader*. *Pacing* involves making your reader feel you and the reader both are *on the same wavelength*. That is, pacing helps your reader feel comfort or rapport with you. Pacing proves rather easy. To pace, simply express

* Similarity
* Agreement
* Understanding

toward your reader.

Third, after you pace your reader, lead your reader. Successful pacing opens up the reader to *leading*. This is "leading" or swaying the comfortable, "on the same wave-length" reader to the conclusions you want. This pacing-and-then-leading method requires that you state the reader's needs (pacing) and then explain how your plan or proposal meets the reader's needs (leading).

Fourth, pace and then lead to overcome your reader's possible objections to your plan or proposal:

　✳ *Pace* by pointing out how each possible objection by your reader holds merit

　✳ Then, *lead* by telling how your plan or proposal handles your reader's objections, resistance, or roadblocks

Fifth, conclude with a bulleted or numbered listing of the *steps* you and/or your reader need to take to carry out your plan or proposal.

A sample memo composed using the 5-Step Persuasive Writing Technique appears on page 191. As you read it, notice where each of the five steps appears.

This memo illustrates the use of the persuasive writing technique that features

Step 1. Beginning with an overview of your *reader's needs.*

Step 2. *Pacing* to make your reader feel that he or she is "on the same wavelength" and comfortable with you, the writer.

Step 3. Using *leading* after pacing your reader.

Step 4. (a) *Stating your reader's possible objections* (pace) and (b) *explaining how your plan handles your reader's possible objections* (lead).

Step 5. Ending with *steps you and your reader needs to take.*

Sample Persuasive Writing Using the 5 Step Persuasive Writing Technique

To: Dana Grant, Manager of Operations

From: Dale Davis, Vice President of Operations

Topic: How to Help Land the Promotion You Want

Over the last year, you and I discussed your career goals many times. You strongly impressed me with how much you want to advance.

As we discussed, I want you to forge ahead. You show an innate ability to figure out how to get things done, and you always follow through to achieve the desired results. Your improvements to our company's bottom line are praiseworthy, indeed.

However, assessments of your advancement potential pinpoint a few skills you need to improve *before* we can deem you promotable. As you know, you need to improve these areas:

* *Smoothly Persuading and Influencing Company Officers.* You do fine influencing your subordinates and peers, but you come across as somewhat insensitive and aggressive with some of our company's officers. It's a fact of life that you must be able to diplomatically sway your future peers (the officers) *before* they can accept you as one of them.

* *Delivering More Dynamic Presentations.* As you mentioned to me, you speak before groups in a too matter-of-fact manner. That style does not promote enthusiasm in your audience. And, let's face it, many decision

makers judge you by how well you deliver presentations.

✳ *Writing Better.* You verbally express yourself quite clearly. Yet, as you pointed out to me, somehow something gets lost when you transfer your ideas to paper.

Dana, I know you are reluctant to take time for outside training in these three skills. You point out you already put in 55- to 60-hour workweeks. Under those circumstances, it is difficult to find time to attend these apparently needed seminars.

At the same time, you tremendously want a promotion. What are your priorities? If you *truly* want to advance, you know it will not occur until you improve in these three high-impact skills.

Given how much you want a promotion—plus how much potential I see in you—it appears you must get your needed training within the next six months. Let's get the ball rolling. Please

1. Enroll in these workshops:

   a. Negotiating, Influencing, and Persuading Workshop

   b. Delivering Impressive Presentations Workshop

   c. Good Business Writing Made Easy Workshop

2. Let me know the dates you will attend each workshop.

3. Meet with me after *each* workshop to discuss *specifically how you will use your new skills on the job.*

Good luck. I feel confident you'll succeed as you usually do.

CHECKLIST—
GOOD BUSINESS WRITING MADE EASY

_____ Just from reading your memo, letter, or report, your reader gets all necessary information. Your reader would not need to ask you for "missing" details.

    _____ Clear, easy to understand

    _____ Logical

    _____ Good spelling, punctuation, and grammar

_____ Use *short*

    _____ Words

    _____ Sentences

_____ *Underline* key words, ideas, or phrases

_____ Use subtitles

_____ Use lists, for example, bulleted or numbered lists

_____ When doing persuasive writing, use *5-Step Persuasive Writing Method*

    _____ Begin with overview of reader's needs

    _____ Pace reader

    _____ Lead

    _____ (a) State reader's possible objections and (b) explain how your plan handles those objections

    _____ End with steps your reader or you need to take

Conclusion

TACTICS TO PUSH *YOUR* SUCCESS TO NEW HEIGHTS

The great goal in life is not knowledge but action.

—Thomas Henry Huxley

Your time to decide has arrived. You must decide exactly how much you want to excel.

You undoubtedly read this book because you feel an inner need. The forcefulness of your urgency is related to how much you want to forge ahead in your career (and probably your nonwork life, too). So you searched this book to uncover how winners do it. Within these pages, you learned the techniques, methods, mind-sets, and the contents of the bag of tricks that high-achievers put into action. These tools help them come out on top in many of their work and nonwork endeavors. After all, as the principle behind *How Winners Do It* clearly lays out:

Being competent in your work
plus 75 cents
will get you a cup of coffee.

Being competent in your work
plus making a fantastic impression on the people who count
will get you at least $100,000 per year.

IT'S NOW UP TO YOU

Now, it is *your* turn. You can make a number of valuable decisions. The easiest road for you is to finish this book, and then just return to behaving as you did before you ever picked it up. If you do this, then this book would have given you only an exercise in mental aerobics. Not changing how you do things will not help you get anywhere you have not already been. As the old adage says,

If you do what you've always done,
then you probably will get what you've
always gotten.

Or, in sharp contrast, *you* now can put this book's pointers and ideas into action. After all, you now know many of the tools winners use.

What you do—or do not do—is totally *your* decision. Realize you can take your new-found knowledge and make your future better than your past.

For readers who feel determined to do it like winners do it, we will now show you how you can

1. Develop your high-impact skills plus

2. Chart your progress with a handy checklist

HOW TO IMPROVE YOUR HIGH-IMPACT SKILLS

You probably know how you stack up in each of the six top skills winners use. Now, let's pinpoint the three main ways you can improve on any of the skills where you need some additional help. These three methods are

* Workshops
* Role models or mentors
* Shadowing

Well-presented *workshops* or seminars help you learn many skills in a fairly short time. You can obtain a heady dose of ideas to use right away in your job and personal life. Buyer beware: Be sure to attend *only* seminars that teach you readily usable skills. Avoid workshops that substitute fluff or academic babble for immediately practical skills.

The *role model* or *mentor* you choose should excel at using one or more skills in which you need to improve. You can watch your role model over a period of time to see first-hand "how to do it." For instance, you can learn how to deliver better presentations by observing a superb presenter or public speaker a number of times. Simply follow this two-step approach with your role models or mentors:

1. *Watch* what your role model or mentor does well.

2. *Copy* or *adapt* the skills you can benefit from.

Be sure to ask them for advice and input. Most people love to give advice, so you actually compliment them when you directly ask for their words of wisdom.

Shadowing is an in-depth way to learn a lot quickly from a role model. Again, pick someone who excels at the skills you need to improve. Then, tag along with that person for one to three days; be as inseparable as possible. Watch how the person operates. For example, one way to learn how to influence others is to shadow a (1) salesperson or (2) executive who coordinates an array of employees into a smoothly functioning team. Observe this person carefully. Pinpoint exactly what behaviors the person uses to succeed. Copy or adapt the techniques that you notice really work.

You can choose among these three ways to learn the high-impact skills you need. However, you must take one absolutely, totally completely crucial action: *You must practice*.

All the wonderful workshops, role models, mentors, and shadowing in the world will not help you unless you practice. This often gets lost in the shuffle. A common reason many people do not practice new skills is because they feel uncomfortable trying them out. The new skills feel unnatural at first. This is true whether the skill is an interpersonal or communications tactic, calculus, or tennis.

As you practice, however, using your new skills proves easier. Eventually, in fact, your new skills become a regular part of your typical everyday behavior. They become totally natural.

CHECKLIST—PLAN AND IMPROVE YOUR HIGH-IMPACT SKILLS

A simple checklist often helps people keep their eyes on a goal and reach it. The same holds true for developing the interpersonal and communications skills you need for your career. The checklist that follows offers you an easy-to-use way to help you plan and monitor your improvements.

High-Impact Skill	Skill Ability			How to Develop Skill			Deadline Date to Develop Skill Well
	Need to Improve	Doing O.K.	Doing Well	Seminar	Role Model	Shadowing	
Quickly make great impression							
Persuading, influencing, and negotiating							
Showmanship							
Delivering impressive presentations							
Conducting highly productive meetings							
Writing crisp, clear, interesting memos, letters, and reports							

NOW YOU CAN DO IT HOW WINNERS DO IT

Now you have it. Between the covers of this book, you possess the action-oriented research, techniques, and pointers that enable ordinary people to transform themselves into extraordinary ones.

The research shows individuals who excel in their careers and rise to the top exude agility in six major communications skills:

* Quickly making a great impression on practically anyone
* Negotiating, influencing, and persuading with suave, diplomatic agility
* Acting out the showmanship high-achievers use so well
* Delivering impressive presentations to any size audience
* Conducting highly productive meetings
* Writing memos, letters, and reports in a crisp, clear, and interesting manner

Importantly, all these skills are totally learnable by any ambitious person. None of these skills that separate high-achievers from underachievers is genetic, inherited, mysterious, or even expensive to learn.

Everyone can shine in these crucial, high-impact skills. You just need to make an honest evaluation of your areas needing improvement. After that, techniques exist at your fingertips to develop all the skills you need so *you* can do it how winners do it.

HOW COMPANIES CAN HELP THEIR EMPLOYEES EXCEL

HOW TO PINPOINT EXACTLY WHICH SKILLS ARE NEEDED

Most executives nod in agreement when asked if superior performance is needed *before* promoting a person into a key position. Of course they agree. Who could disagree? Yet these same executives very often do not know what skills indicate potential to do well, that is, be a winner in various positions. Or, more exactly, executives fairly easily spot an employee's strengths and weaknesses in technical competencies, but they find it much more difficult to pinpoint which interpersonal or communications skills employees lack that will keep those employees from zooming ahead in their careers.

Fortunately, a few methods exist to point the way—to unravel exactly what an employee needs to do to forge ahead in his or her career. These methods include the following:

* Personality and mental ability assessments geared to predict career potential
* Management development planning meetings
* Performance appraisals

This appendix considers how companies can enhance their employees' potential using these methods. Importantly, after reading about each method, you get a peek into case examples.

PROFITING FROM PSYCHOLOGICAL ASSESSMENTS OF CAREER POTENTIAL

Everyone would love to own a crystal ball. The crystal ball would let you see the future, and you could profit from such spectacular foresight. Unfortunately, crystal balls do not yet exist.

However, there is a certain type of scientific prediction method that can help companies and their employees. These are psychologically oriented assessments of individuals done by industrial psychologists. Such business-oriented psychological assessments can help to (1) forecast career potential of current employees and (2) predict on-the-job success of job applicants.[1]

These assessments focus on the individual's ability to successfully carry out job duties. They do *not* focus on mental health or illness. They are conducted by *industrial* psychologists who specialize in the psychology of organizational success.

Such assessments usually are conducted on candidates for executive, managerial, sales, and professional positions.

---

[1]For a more in-depth explanation of such testing and assessments, you may want to refer to another of my books, *Hire the Best and Avoid the Rest*.

Some companies also have assessments done of current incumbents who serve in those same kinds of positions for the purpose of evaluating and developing their potential.

Here, we will focus on assessments of current employees (incumbents) who a company may want to consider for a promotion or other career development. (This discussion will not deal with assessing job candidates who do not work for the company, although many of the same assessment methods are used.)

The assessment process requires four steps:

Step 1. *Hold a discussion with the executive for whom the employee works.* This discussion gives the industrial psychologist crucial information about what would be required of the person being assessed. This discussion should cover the (1) positions for which the employee is being considered for a promotion or lateral move and (2) the corporate culture, that is, what it takes to do well in the organization's particular interpersonal environment or "culture." Other key executives in the company also may speak with the psychologist about these same two issues.

Step 2. *Assess employee.* The assessment includes two parts: (1) tests and (2) a two- to four-hour in-depth interview. The psychologist uses this same rigorous procedure for each person he or she assesses.

Step 3. *Discuss employee's assessment with key executives.* About one-half hour to one hour after the testing and lengthy interview ends, the psychologist phones the executive for whom the employee works and, if appropriate, other key executives. The psychologist presents his or evaluation and recommendations on the employee.

Step 4. *Provide a typed assessment report.* The psychologist writes up the assessment and sends it to the key executives who are concerned about the employee's development and career potential. The assessment report contains two main parts:

* Evaluation of Employee

* Recommendations to Management

The Evaluation of Employee section usually covers topics related to the person's on-the-job success, such as the following:

* Motivation

* Problem-solving approach (intellectual skills)

* Communications skills

* Management or sales style (depending on the position for which person is being considered)

* Approach to work

* Approach to people

* Interests

* Personality and temperament

Sample Psychological Assessment of Career Potential

The following is a psychological assessment of a company's manager who is being considered for promotion to an executive position. As you will notice, the *Recommendations to Management* section includes four suggestions for how this employee could improve his potential.

This employee's weaknesses definitely were not in his technical skills. Instead, his major weaknesses or areas that needed improvement centered on his interpersonal and communications skills. Therefore, recommendations for this employee included

- ✴ giving the employee direct feedback on his interpersonal skills
- ✴ setting up a planning and follow-up method with his boss to help him carry out each recommendation
- ✴ training him in negotiating skills
- ✴ teaching him in how to write better memos, letters, and reports

Interestingly, this employee and his boss proved quite diligent in following up on each of the recommendations made in the assessment. About a year after the assessment, when an appropriate vice presidency opened up in the company, he got it!

Importantly, until this assessment was done, his boss and other executives thought he probably possessed the potential to advance, but did not know how to direct him. The assessment pointed the way. The employee knew where he needed to improve, and his employer was able to help him develop into a valued executive.

Sample Assessment of Career Potential

Employee: Mr. R

Current Position: Director of Industrial Engineering

Evaluation of Employee

Motivations

Mr. R possesses an average to above-average level of drive and ambition. His greatest motivation is to achieve results. His strongest enjoyment in his job centers on accomplishing his goals. He also craves recognition for his expertise and problem-solving abilities. Mr. R likes people to spot what he does and pay special attention to him for it.

He also greatly values tackling challenges in a creative manner. He plays with ideas and likes coming up with new, unique ways of looking at situations and getting things done. Mr. R is somewhat of a trainer or teacher at heart. He relishes sharing his knowledge with others. This markedly adds to Mr. R's level of self-esteem.

He likes to get quite heavily involved in his work. However, due to his somewhat cerebral approach, his work may not be immediately noticeable since he tends to do a lot of his work "in his head," before he takes action. As a result, people may perceive him as someone who works in a somewhat quiet manner.

<u>Problem-Solving Approach</u>

Mr. R takes a very analytical approach to dissecting and solving problems. As mentioned, Mr. R can seem rather cerebral; that is, he thinks a lot before he puts his solutions into action. This results in Mr. R taking a slow, steady, somewhat plodding approach to surveying how to tackle projects.

Given his strongly analytical thinking style, he is quite a data collector. Mr. R gathers together all the bits and pieces of a problem and then slowly dissects the situation before he commits himself to a mode of action.

On the other hand, Mr. R is rather innovative. This is particularly interesting, because very detail-focused people—such as Mr. R—generally are not imaginative thinkers. However, as noted, Mr. R is rather motivated to do creative work. Thus, with his combined, creativity motivation and thinking style, he does well at (1) playing with ideas and methods, (2) transcending standard operating procedures, and (3) conjuring up new ways to handle problems.

Communications Skills

Mr. R tends to express himself in a brief, to-the-point manner. However, he often fails to explain his ideas, or their rationale or background, until someone asks him to do so. Along the same line, Mr. R sometimes tosses out terms or jargon without making sure the person he is talking to understands what he means. Such tendencies can promote miscommunications and misunderstandings.

He listens fairly well, although he sometimes ventures off on tangents unrelated to the questions or comments posed to him. When asked a question, Mr. R often pauses before he answers and stares at his questioner while thinking about his response. Although he is thinking, this idiosyncrasy makes Mr. R seem to be staring right through the person he is addressing.

His writing lacks fluidity. Mr. R puts thoughts on paper in a somewhat "smorgasbord" fashion, dabbling a little in one thought and then a little in another. His writing dances around and takes awhile to zero in on the main point he wants to make. As a result, his writing exhibits less focus than it should.

Management Style

Mr. R relishes collaborating with others and using teamwork. He particularly enjoys cooperating with others on joint projects and assignments. However, he does so with an intense focus on the technical and engineering factors, with only passing concern for the personal or emotional aspects involved in collaborating.

He works hard when he manages projects. However, a drawback is his overriding concern with achieving technical results. He does not seem to have a particularly strong desire to handle the interpersonal components of management. Instead, this is something he does out of necessity, rather than out of an urge to do so.

Mr. R relishes teaching and training, and he puts great effort into showing people how to work smarter.

Interpersonal Skills

He does not go out of his way to warm up to people he has just met. As someone who often seems fairly wrapped up in his own thoughts, Mr. R focuses on his own concerns noticeably more than the concerns, ideas, goals or feelings of people around him. Due to this tendency, Mr. R comes off as more of a technician than a people-oriented human being. Adding to this interpersonal approach is the fact that Mr. R expresses minimal empathy for others' personal concerns.

Mr. R does not always show awareness of social norms. He sometimes does not take into account how others might expect him to act in particular situations. He would not act rude. However, he can come across as less than fully poised and polished.

Personality and Temperament

This is a basically calm, rational fellow. He feels rather uncomfortable in conflict situations and prefers to avoid them.

Mr. R exudes a moderate level of energy. He certainly can act quite unemotional. In fact, he frequently seems rather "poker faced" in that he shows little reaction or emotion in his facial expression. He is not a person given to acting animated and spontaneous.

Most people tend to display either a predominantly positive mental attitude or a mainly negative mental attitude. However, given his exceedingly rational demeanor, Mr. R comes off relatively neutral in terms of his general outlook on life. Yet, inside, he does have more feelings than he lets the outside world know. Nevertheless, he keeps them to himself as he shows the world a strongly rational, straightforward personality.

Recommendations to Management

We consider Mr. R an average candidate for promotion to the position of Vice President of Industrial Engineering. This is based on how well he fits the sort of attributes your company needs in an executive holding that role. However, Mr. R can take certain actions to improve his ability to potentially move into this vice president role. Recommendations of the specific actions Mr. R should take to improve key skills are presented near the end of this report. First, this report summarizes his (1) strengths and (2) weaknesses or areas needing improvement.

Strengths

On the positive side, Mr. R possesses some fine talents. He is a keenly results-focused manager. This is his strongest asset. Mr. R also is quite analytical, so he thinks through problems in a finely honed, detailed manner.

Furthermore, this fellow also proves quite innovative. He shows much curiosity about applying technology in unique ways. All in all, Mr. R is a real "thinker."

Also on the plus side, it should be noted that Mr. R shows avid interest in training others. He relishes conveying his knowledge and insights to others. That is one key element your company seeks in all its vice presidents, including its Vice President of Industrial Engineering.

Weaknesses or Areas Needing Improvement

On the other side of the coin, however, Mr. R is more technically oriented than people oriented. Such strong technical leanings work well in lower- and middle-management positions, like jobs Mr. R has held so far in his career. However, to succeed in an executive-level position, such as vice president of your company, an effective person also must exhibit many sharp interpersonal and communications skills.

This is where Mr. R falls short of the optimal candidate for your Vice President of Industrial Engineering position. People play second fiddle to technology in his view. Also, Mr. R sometimes comes off as too wrapped up in himself. As such, he possesses a too limited amount of the tact and "people smarts" your company desires and needs in its executives.

He displays only a moderate degree of empathy, warmth, and sensitivity. For example, Mr. R exerts minimal effort "reading" people so he could figure out how to work best with each individual's personality. This also limits how well he could negotiate with or persuade people, since those crucial executive skills would require him to help people feel comfortable and in rapport with him.

Also, to put it bluntly, Mr. R's writing skills need sharpening. Executives need to quickly "tell people what time it is"; Mr. R tends to "tell people how to build a clock" when he write memos, letters, and reports. He needs to learn to organize his writing so he gets to the point. Also, adding a little flair to his phrasing would help him appear more confident and personable in his writings.

Recommendations to Help Mr. R Improve on Crucial Skills

If your company decides to develop Mr. R into a person who could hold an executive-level position, then the following suggestions could help him:

1. *Encourage his creativity*

   It is one of the biggest assets he brings to your company. Also, it is frequently not found to such a large degree in employees who work in extremely technical specialties.

2. *Give Mr. R clear feedback on how he comes across to people, that is, his interpersonal skills*

He especially needs to know how his people skills thwart his advancement potential. While doing this may feel somewhat uncomfortable, it would prove very helpful for Mr. R's boss and other executives to sit down with him in private and give Mr. R direct—yet sensitive—feedback on how he comes across to others. Make sure that these feedback sessions are done only one-on-one and that Mr. R realizes such feedback is to help him improve his potential for advancement. Within one week after these feedback sessions, Mr. R's boss needs to meet with him to

a. List the feedback comments Mr. R received

b. List exactly what actions Mr. R can take day to day to improve how he comes across to others

Discussions between Mr. R and his boss on his progress in improving these skills need to take place at least monthly for six months. Such follow-up discussions show Mr. R that (1) the company is serious about helping him develop much-needed skills and (2) he must keep on track so that when an executive position opens up for which he may be suitable, he will get serious attention.

3. *Send Mr. R to a negotiating workshop and then follow up*

He certainly could use improvement in this key executive skill. After attending this workshop, Mr. R's boss should meet with him to discuss what Mr. R learned and to add those negotiating skills to the list they developed during recommendation 1.

4. *Send Mr. R to a writing skills workshop and then follow up*

He needs to improve his written communications. Since Mr. R gains a lot from classroom instruction, seminars on business writing skills would give him the tools he needs to express his thoughts better on paper.

It also is suggested that your company have Mr. R meet one-on-one with the writing skills trainer two times following the workshop:

* 2 weeks later

* 2 months later

These one-on-one coaching sessions should help Mr. R get professional feedback and advice on how to further improve his writing skills.

This <u>Evaluation and Recommendations</u> for Mr. R Were Prepared for Your Company By

Michael W. Mercer, Ph.D.
Industrial Psychologist

BENEFITING FROM MANAGEMENT DEVELOPMENT PLANNING MEETINGS

Executives can wield a tremendously powerful sword in their drive to develop management talent. This "sword" is a management development planning (MDP) meeting.

What Are MDP Meetings?

These meetings take place once or twice a year, preferably twice. They are called by the top-ranking executive in a company or each of its divisions. The corporate-level MDP meetings are called by the company president or chief executive, and participants are everyone who reports directly to that person. Also, each division needs to hold its own MDP meeting, led by the division's general manager, with everybody reporting to the general manager also participating.

What Goes on in MDP Meetings?

A facilitator, usually an industrial psychologist or perhaps a management development specialist, leads the MDP meeting. During MDP meetings, the participants discuss every manager in their company or division in terms of each manager's

* Strengths
* Weaknesses
* Specific skills the manager must develop before being considered for a promotion or transfer to a more challenging position

Perhaps the most important topic is the last one mentioned, namely, laying out what specific skills each manager must develop *before* possibly earning a promotion or other career move. This is decided by *group concensus*. How? All participants must openly comment on their observations and interactions with each manager. Such open discussion helps draw a picture of how each manager performs in a variety of work relationships.

For instance, one manager may perform quite admirably in her department plus some other departments. However, in one or two departments this same manager may be perceived as gruff, abrasive, and a pain to deal with. That provides crucial insights into the manager's *style* and *impact*. Without input from *all* department executives, such a complete picture could not be drawn. Only a lopsided, incomplete picture would exist.

Sample Management Development Planning Meeting Evaluation and Follow-up

One manager discussed in a MDP meeting was Ms. S. She possessed excellent technical skills and a real talent for rallying her staff to complete projects (1) before their due dates and (2) delightfully under budget.

However, Ms. S also evidenced certain problems, including

1. Trouble getting along with the vice president of her department.

2. Butting heads with managers in other divisions, including acting bullheaded when visiting them while completing projects.

3. Writing that was quite precise but proved too detailed and lacked any colorful flair to make it interesting to read.

Ms. S's management problems readily translate into certain high-impact skills discussed in this book. These problems are Ms. S's difficulties in

1. Developing rapport and creating a good impression on people who could make or break her career

2. Persuading, influencing, and negotiating smoothly and diplomatically with people over whom she could not exert any formal authority

3. Writing in a crisp, clear, interesting manner

To help Ms. S, she received specific training and coaching in her three main problem areas. Beginning with, *to develop rapport and create a great impression on important people*, Ms. S learned the *4 Interpersonal Styles* method to succeeding with people. For instance, Ms. S was detail-focused, yet her vice president came off as friendly-focused. This was evident by the vice president's golf posters and memorabilia in his office, and his consistent tendency to smile and chit-chat. Ms. S received instruction on how to *act* more friendly-focused with her vice president. It took some effort but she worked her way onto his good side.

Ms. S also experienced trouble *developing rapport with people she had just met*. She came across as rather uptight and too work oriented. To solve this problem, she began applying the *4 Interpersonal Styles* method, plus lots of practice mirroring and asking open-ended questions. Ms. S also tried some good, old-fashioned smiling when she dealt with people, especially people she just met. By doing these things, she began to come across as warmer, and she began to lose her "cold" image.

Next, Ms. S's *negotiating, influencing, and persuading skills needed beefing up*. Flaunting her I-Know-I'm-Right demeanor, she turned off people she needed to influence. After all, much of being a successful manager is smoothly and subtly influencing people over whom the manager exerts no formal control.

Difficulty in swaying others spells the kiss of death in management circles.

To help Ms. S, she was guided through a two-pronged approach. First, she attended a *How to Negotiate, Influence, and Persuade Workshop*. Second, Ms. S "shadowed" another manager who exhibited superb persuasion skills. She followed him for two half-days to watch how he influenced others. She then could use this successful manager as a role model and copy his agile negotiating style.

Additionally, Ms. S needed to overcome the third flaw holding her back, namely, her detail-focused *dreary writing style*. To correct this problem, she attended the *Good Business Writing Made Easy Workshop*. She also later met twice with the writing instructor to review her writing and check up on her progress. Given this training and one-to-one coaching, Ms. S's writing style took on a bouncier, more colorful tinge, while appropriately conveying the finely honed details she held so very dear.

All in all, Ms. S posed a thorny problem. Her innate abilities, analytical mind, and strong drive made her chock-full of potential. But she needed to soften some rough edges. She needed to enhance her ability at (1) quickly developing rapport; (2) negotiating, influencing, and persuading; and (3) writing in a crisper, more enjoyable-to-read manner. Using workshops, "shadowing" a role model, one-to-one coaching, and lots of effort, Ms. S succeeded. The executives around her noticed the improvements. They began viewing Ms. S. in a vastly more favorable light.

This came out in subsequent MDP meetings. Eventually, she earned her stripes and achieved the promotion she sought.

HOW TO *REALLY* HELP EMPLOYEES THROUGH PERFORMANCE APPRAISALS

An annual event more foreboding than taxes lurks in practically every employee's life. It is the yearly performance appraisal or review. That occurs when a person's previous 12 months of endeavors come under scrutiny by his or her boss.

All too often, the performance review smacks of blatantly subjective judgments. It also usually concludes with rather vague, half-hearted suggestions to improve performance.

As a result, performance appraisals hold tremendous room for upgrading. One improvement is to insist that *specific* problems in performance *be stated* and *specific* solutions given. Do away with wishy-washy, semiserious "suggestions" for improving performance. Instead, performance reviews need clearly laid-out areas in which the employee needs improvement, as well as equally clear ways to develop those needed skills.

SAMPLE PERFORMANCE APPRAISAL

The executive who supervised Mr. W felt the skills presented in this book were highly relevant for *all* managers to master. She reviewed each of her subordinates with an eye
toward how well (or poorly) they demonstrated the high-
impact skills needed to accomplish their work goals.

Mr. W represented a particularly thorny problem. He
hung onto each of his jobs by dogged hard work, fierce deter-
mination, and an overriding willingness to please. Indeed, he
had always done well as he progressed in his career at the
company.

Yet his next step would launch him into a company officer role. His visibility in the company and in its community
would increase many times over as soon as he became a vice
president.

That was where the problem arose. Mr. W always did
well as an "inside" man. He maneuvered smoothly inside his
division, and he used his friendly, sensitive, good-humored
nature to make it hard for people not to like him.

Yet he was not sufficiently presentable to the world outside his division. "Right now," his boss explained, "he just
couldn't represent the company to the outside world."

Why? Because his ability to deliver *presentations* in
front of groups left much to be desired. Also, he lacked certain make-it-or-break-it *showmanship* skills. These deficits
were duly noted in his annual performance appraisal. Also,
Mr. W was told in no uncertain terms that either he shaped
up in these two arenas, or he could forget about any further
promotion potential.

Mr. W dove into tackling his presentation skills and
showmanship problems. To enhance his public speaking ability, Mr. W took the *Delivering Impressive Presentations
Workshop*. He found people to help him make splendid

transparencies and slides. Mr. W also attended presentations by some of his company's best public speakers so he could study superb presenters firsthand. This helped him pinpoint specific behaviors of role models who knew how to shine.

Next, Mr. W sought candid feedback on his showmanship traits. He interviewed his supervisor plus a few other company officers. Mr. W asked them what showmanship skills he needed to improve. From this frank feedback, he learned he needed to change his style of dress and way of talking.

To begin with, Mr. W's suits, ties, shirts, and shoes just did not fit in with the company officer's normal mode of dress. His clothes were out of date for the very up-to-date, fashion-consciousness of the company's officers (his future *peers*, he hoped). Also, most company officers wore business suits or dresses in shades of blue and gray. In contrast, Mr. W favored shades of brown and tan. Stemming from this feedback, Mr. W began noticing for the first time in his life how the top executives dressed. He never paid much attention before. Clothes previously just did not interest him. That changed dramatically. Mr. W began drinking in the clothing styles and colors of the company officers he wanted to emulate. He bought himself a new wardrobe for the office and donated his old duds to charity.

Finally, Mr. W was told by a few executives, in addition to his boss, that he had one habit that really annoyed executives. Specifically, he talked too much about himself and too infrequently asked others about themselves. As Mr. W explained, he came across "more wrapped up in me than in other people. I acted self-absorbed. It wasn't done on purpose. I just never realized that most people would rather talk about themselves than listen to me go on and on talking about myself. I found out that wasn't true."

Mr. W's actions helped him progress quickly and quite noticeably. During a company reorganization, a vice president slot opened up. Mr. W readily stepped into it. Shortly after his ascension, he mentioned, "That last performance appraisal opened up my eyes. I had never seen so clearly how I came across. I might have pouted or just pooh-poohed my so-called presentation and showmanship deficiencies. But I took the bull by the horns. I personally researched what I did wrong and I figured out how to wind up on top!"

INDEX

A

Agreement, 84-85, *see also*
  Verbal agreements
Appraisals, *see also* Assessment
  of employee performance, 216
  sample, 217-19
Artful vagueness, 43-46
  defusing anger by, 46-48
  and hard-to-please audiences,
    129-30
Assessment, *see also* Appraisals
  of employee career potential,
    202-4
  employee evaluation sample,
    205-12
  psychological, 204-5
Attitudes
  accentuating positive, 89-93
  exuding confidence, 93-96
  positive vs. negative, 90
  team player, 96-97
Audio-visual aids, for presenta-
    tions, 120-23

B

Business writing, 163-64, *see also*
  Writing skills
  checklist for, 193
  costs of, 164-65
  and detail-focused reader,
    168-69
  and friendly-focused reader,
    168, 170
  informative writing tech-
    niques, 188
  outlining, 171-73
  and partying-focused reader,
    170-71
  persuasive writing techniques,
    189-92
  and reader-oriented language,
    170-71
  "read" the reader's needs,
    167-68
  and results-focused reader,
    168
  sample five-step persuasive
    technique, 191-92

steps in, 172
types of, 188-92
winning appearance of, 167
Buy low, sell high, 72-74

C

Career assessment, 202-10
Career-limiting moves
high-achievers and, 100
inappropriate behavior, 101-2
topics to avoid, 101-3
underachievers and, 100
Charm, 5
Checklist
for business writing, 193
for conducting productive
meetings, 162
for delivering presentations,
137-38
for good business writing, 193
for high-impact skill 1, 51
for high-impact skill 2, 86-87
for high-impact skill 3, 107
for high-impact skill 4, 137-38
for high-impact skill 5, 162
for high-impact skill 6, 193
for how to negotiate, 86-87
for improving high-impact
skills, 198-99
for making a great impression,
51
for showmanship, 107
Comfort
finding similarities and, 14
indicators, 13
and making great impression,
11-15

Platinum Rule and, 14-15
putting people at ease, 11-15,
22
Communications skills, 200
Compliments
high-achievers and, 106
importance of paying, 49-50
underachievers and, 106
Contract, 84-85, *see also* Verbal
agreements
Costs
of business writing, 164-65
of meetings, 142-44

D

Detail-focused meetings, 149
Detail-focused people, 16-23,
168-69
Dress code, 37-38

E

Employees
assessing career potential of,
202-10
evaluation criteria, 204-10
improving skills of, 201-19
and performance appraisals,
216-19
pinpointing skills needed by,
201-2
recommendations to help,
210-12
sample career assessment,
204-10
sample performance appraisal,
217-19

F

Friendly-focused meetings, 149
Friendly-focused people, 16-19,
  22-23, 168, 170

H

High-achievers, *see also* High-
  impact skills
  attitudes of, 89-91
  compared with underachiev-
    ers, 1-4, 89-91
  and publicizing successes, 98-
    100
  skills of, 4-8
  and taking responsibility, 97-
    98
  and teamwork, 96-97
High-impact skill 1, *see also*
  Interpersonal styles
  artful vagueness, 43-48, 129-
    30
  checklist for, 51
  impressing nervous people, 22
  listening technique, 38-41
  making a great impression, 5,
    15-41
  making people comfortable,
    11-15
  mirror technique, 24-38
  paying compliments, 49-50
  recognizing interpersonal
    styles, 16-24
  using names, 48-49
High-impact skill 2, *see also*
  Negotiation techniques
  checklist for, 86-87
  dangers of verbal agreements,
    83-85

getting people to agree with
  you, 63-65
how to conclude every negotiation, 85
never use "Why," 69-70
the "Or" technique, 65-66
overcoming resistance, 66-69
persuasion skills, 56-63
salesmanship, 5-6
surefire negotiating techniques, 71-83
win-win negotiation, 53-54
High-impact skill 3, *see also*
  Attitudes
  accentuating the positive, 89-
    93
  assuming total responsibility,
    97-98
  avoiding career-limiting
    moves, 100-103
  avoiding stressing others, 104-6
  checklist for, 107
  exuding confidence, 93-96
  paying compliments daily, 106
  publicizing your successes, 98-
    100
  teamwork, 96-97
High-impact skill 4, *see also*
  Presentations
  ability to motivate, 6
  body movement, 124-25
  checklist for, 137-38
  copying professional speakers,
    125-26
  delivering dynamic presenta-
    tions, 110-12
  encouraging/controlling audi-
    ence participation, 131-32
  giving persuasive presenta-
    tions, 135-36

how to feel calm and confident, 112-15

how to prepare presentations,
116-23

making informative presentations, 134-35

maximum impact voice use,
125

tackling difficult questions,
126-30

what not to say, 132-34

High-impact skill 5, *see also*
Meetings

checklist for, 162

conducting productive meetings, 139-40

how to have a successful
meeting, 144-61

presentation ability, 6-7

what a meeting is, 140-44

High-impact skill 6, *see also*
Business writing; Writing

business writing types, 188-92

checklist for, 193

effective writing skills, 163-67

good business writing, 167-72

writing ability, 7

writing like a winner, 172-88

High-impact skills, 4-5

improvement checklist, 198-99

improving your, 197-98

translating skills into action,
195-96

Hourglass phenomenon, 150-51

I

Impact, 8

and success, 111

Impression, *see also* Comfort;
High-impact skill 1

making great, 11-51

Improvement

of high-impact skills, 198-99

methods for, 197-200

sample recommendations for,
210-12

workshops for, 197

Influence, *see* Negotiation

Interpersonal styles

detail-focused, 16-23

friendly-focused, 16-19, 22-23

guidelines for dealing with,
22-24

partying-focused, 16, 18, 20, 22

quick quiz on, 19-20

results-focused, 16-23

using the technique, 20-22

L

Listening technique, 38-41

productive listening, 40-41

Lose-lose negotiation, 53-54

Lose-lose situation, exiting from,
79

M

Management development planning (MDP) meetings, 212

agenda of, 213

sample evaluation of, 213-16

MDP, *see* Management development planning

Meetings, *see also* MDP meetings

agenda for, 147-48

announcement memos for, 146-47

and the Arguer, 152, 154

audience participation in, 154-56

and bottom line, 141-44

characteristics of productive meetings, 144-45

checklist for, 162

conducting, 148-60

cost-benefit analysis of, 142-44

cost of, 142-44

creating productive tone for, 149-50

description of, 140-41

detail-focused, 149

friendly-focused, 149

goals for, 146

how to conclude, 160

informative, 157

leadership role in, 150-54

main reason for, 141-44

MDP, 212-16

and the Motormouth, 152-53

and participants' key senses, 151-52

partying-focused, 149-50

persuasive, 157-58

physical environment for, 148-49

planning, 145-47

postmeeting follow-up, 161

problem-solving, 157, 159-60

productive tone for, 149-50

productive vs unproductive, 139-40

results-focused, 149

Ringmaster role in, 140, 144-61

and the Scare Crow, 152-53

and the Silent One, 152-53

steps for success in, 145-61

troublesome participants in, 152-54

types of, 157-60

Memos

    to detail-focused reader, 168-69

    to friendly-focused reader, 168, 170

    to partying-focused reader, 170-71

    to results-focused reader, 168

Mentors

    and skills improvement, 197, 199

Mirror technique

    and attire, 34-38, *see also* Dress code

    and body language, 24-29

    in meetings, 31-32

    mirroring power, 29-32

    and vocal style, 32-34

N

Negotiation, *see also* Persuasion skills

    conclusion of, 85

    overcoming resistance in, 66-69

    two-step method of, 54-56

    verbal agreement dangers in, 83-85

Negotiation outcomes

    lose-lose, 53-54

    win-lose, 54

    win-win, 54-56, 71, 73-75

Negotiation techniques
  back burner tactic, 79
  backscratching, 83
  brainstorming, 76
  fait accompli approach, 77-78
  FBI technique, 80
  higher authority, 78-79
  Robin Hood, 71-74
  time-is-on-your-side, 74-75
  Tom Sawyer, 76-77
  ultimatum, 80-81
  vanish technique, 81-83

O

Open-ended questions vs. closed-
  ended questions, 59-63

P

Partying-focused meetings, 149-
  50
Partying-focused people, 16, 18,
  20, 22, 170-71
Performance appraisal, 217-19,
  see also Assessment
Persuasion skills, *see also*
  Negotiation
  ask for what you want, 56
  ask the "right" questions, 58-
  63
  pace-and-then-lead technique,
  57-58
  persuasive writing, 189-92
Platinum Rule, 14-15, 21
Presentations, *see also* High-
  impact skill 4
  ability in, 6-7

  audience expectations of, 110-
  12
  audience participation in, 131-
  32
  audio-visual aids for, 120-23
  checklist for delivering, 137-38
  DOs of, 124-26
  and hard-to-please audiences,
  126-30
  impressive, 109-10
  informative, 134-35
  organizing, 119-120
  persuasive, 135-36
  and promotion, 109-10
  "reading" the audience in,
  116-19
  showmanship in, 121, 125-26
  tackling difficult questions in,
  126-30
  techniques for preparing, 116-
  23
  types of, 134-36
  using humor in, 115
  what *not* to say, 132-34
Promotion
  assessments and, 202-12
  MDP meeting evaluation and,
  213-16
  performance appraisals and,
  217-19
  presentations and, 109-10
  showmanship and, 89-106
  skills needed for, 191-92, 197-
  98

R

Resistance, how to overcome, 66-
  69

Responsibility, assuming total, 97-98

Results-focused meetings, 149

Results-focused people 16-23,168

Ringmaster, 6

and meetings, 140-61

S

Salesmanship, 5

Shadowing, 6

and skills improvement, 198-99

Showmanship, 6, *see also* High-impact skill 3

checklist for, 107

high-achievers vs under-achievers, 98-100

in presentations, 121, 125-26

and promotions, 89-106

Skills improvement, 201-19

mentors and, 197, 199

persuasion, 56-63

shadowing and, 198-99

workshops and, 197, 199

Stress

high-achievers and, 104

inappropriate relief of, 104-6

Style, 8, *see also* Interpersonal style

and success, 111

Success

expanding, 195-200

publicizing, 98-100

and style, 111

Success magazine, 5

T

Teamwork, 96-97

Techniques

for adding color to writing, 181-82

artful vagueness, 43-48

back burner routine, 79

backscratching, 83

brainstorming tactic, 76

bullets for easy reading, 186-87

for delivering presentations, 112-15

fait accompli approach, 77-78

FBI, 80

for feeling calm/confident, 112-15

higher authority, 78-79

K.I.S.S., 175

listening attentively, 38-43

mirror technique, 24-38

for negotiating, 54-63, 71-83

"or" technique, 65-66

for overcoming resistance, 66-69

pace-then-lead, 54-56

paying compliments, 49-50

for persuasive writing, 189-92

for preparing great presenta-tions, 116-23

P.S. for attention, 184

for recognizing interpersonal styles, 16-24

Robin Hood, 71-74

speeded-up outlining, 173

subtitling, 185

time-is-on-your-side tactic, 74-75

Tom Sawyer tactic, 76-77
ultimatum, 80-81
underlining, 184-85
using names, 48-49
vanish, 81-83
for vibrant writing, 176-80

U

Underachievers, 2-4, *see also*
High-achievers
attitudes of, 89-90
and publicizing successes, 98-
100

V

Verbal agreements, dangers of,
83-85

W

Win-lose negotiation, 54
Win-lose situation, exiting from,
79
Winners, *see also* High-impact
skills 1-6
attitudes of, 90-100
communications skills of, 200
how they do it, 2-5
Win-win negotiation, 54-56
Win-win outcome
backscratching technique and,
83

FBI technique and, 80
Robin Hood technique and, 73
time-is-on-your-side technique
and, 74-75
ultimatums and, 80-81
vanish technique and, 82-83
Words to avoid, 69-70
Workshops, and skills improvement, 197, 199
Writing, *see also* Business writing
adding color to, 181-82
adding spice to, 179
benefiting from bullets, 186-87
converting passive phrases to
active phrases, 180
creating visual impact, 187-88
dread of, 166-67
faster and better, 171-72
freewriting technique, 171-72
informative writing, 188
K.I.S.S. your reader, 175-76
like a winner, 172-88
passive verbs to avoid, 177
persuasive writing, 189-92
P.S. as attention-getter, 184
speeded-up outlining, 173
subtitles for clarity, 185
underline to help reader, 184-
85
using vibrant words, 176-80
words focusing on reader's
needs, 182-84
Writing skills, 163-92, *see also*
Business writing